PRAISE FOR

SEX, LIES AND THE BALLOT BOX

)IAN POLITICS BOOKS OF THE YEAR, *SUNDAY TIMES* POLITICS BOOKS OF
E YEAR, *INDEPENDENT ON SUNDAY* POLITICS BOOKS OF THE YEAR,
ADDY POWER PRACTICAL POLITICS BOOK OF THE YEAR SHORTLIST

is book is such an utterly brilliant idea it is ridiculous that no one has
thought of it before. I cannot recommend it highly enough.'
– JOHN RENTOUL

mart, funny and illuminating in ways you could never dream of.'
– EMILY MAITLIS

'[A] wonderful book of political well-I-nevers.'
– *THE INDEPENDENT*

years I've toyed with writing a *Freakonomics*-style book that translates
olitical academics know ... Philip Cowley and Robert Ford have beaten
it ... Worse, they and the many authors of *Sex, Lies and the Ballot Box*
one a good job of it. The book's 51 chapters are very wide-ranging, and
full of great nuggets of information.'
– PETER CUTHBERTSON, CONSERVATIVEHOME.COM

'The political book that everybody's talking about.'
– MIKE SMITHSON, POLITICALBETTING.COM

s *and the Ballot Box* is a revelation, a paperback with an eye-catching
ad essays by 51 political scientists ... superb and eminently quotable.'
– *THE TIMES*

Lies and the Ballot Box is as entertaining as it is thought-provoking.'
– *INDEPENDENT ON SUNDAY*

'It does it with such aplomb that no political home's Christmas tree should be without a copy neatly wrapped and waiting beneath it.'
– PROGRESS

'This knits academic research with accessible and thought-provoking questions. If you love elections you'll be hooked.'
– MAIL ON SUNDAY

'Finally, the one book you need before the election. This is a wonderfully eclectic collection of academic research translated into normal English. I can pay no higher tribute to it than to say that someone I know supported votes at 16 until he read the short chapter on the subject. This book may not change your life but it may change your mind.'
– THE INDEPENDENT (POLITICS BOOKS OF 2014)

'*Freakonomics* for political junkies. The perfect book for anyone with even a passing interest in politics.'
– DAILY EXPRESS

'If you want to know why people lie about voting, when racism stopped being normal, and whether attractive candidates get more votes then this is most definitely the book for you.'
– LIB DEM VOICE

'A terrific book … Anyone interested in voting and elections would find it enlightening. If I could make it compulsory reading for people who follow my blog, I would…'
– THE GUARDIAN

'It is possible to gain a firmer grasp of the manifold peculiarities that pervade UK elections. I can recommend no better way of doing so than to read *Sex, Lies and the Ballot Box*.'
– DEMOCRATIC AUDIT UK

MORE SEX, LIES'
& THE BALLOT BOX

ANOTHER 50 THINGS
YOU NEED TO KNOW
ABOUT ELECTIONS

EDITED BY
PHILIP COWLEY & ROBERT FORD

FOREWORD BY
ISABEL HARDMAN

First published in Great Britain in 2016 by
Biteback Publishing Ltd
Westminster Tower
3 Albert Embankment
London SE1 7SP

ISBN 978-1-78590-090-7

10 9 8 7 6 5 4 3 2 1

A CIP catalogue record for this book is available from the British Library.

Set in Minion Pro by Adrian McLaughlin

Printed and bound in Great Britain by
CPI Group (UK) Ltd, Croydon CR0 4YY

MIX
Paper from
responsible sources
FSC
www.fsc.org
FSC® C020471

Contents

Foreword

Isabel Hardman

One of the features of the EU referendum campaign was leading politicians being lectured in their TV debates by English Literature graduates. These students of words claimed that their degrees had given them a special insight into whether someone was producing waffle.

Their questions to David Cameron and Michael Gove reminded me of my own English Literature professor at university, who turned around to us at the start of one semester and told us: 'You're second-year students, so you have mastered the art of talking your way through a whole seminar without reading the book. And I am now a professor, so I have mastered the art of teaching an entire module without having read it either.'

Politics often feels the same: in a game that boils down to hard numbers, its participants (including this English Literature graduate) can get away with a tremendous amount of waffle without having read the book.

2015 wasn't a great year for political punditry. If the combined weight of our political predictions had the power to come true, Ed Miliband would be Prime Minister in a minority government backed up by the SNP by now, and Jeremy Corbyn would be continuing to potter about his allotment in relative political obscurity.

Given we managed to survive getting nearly everything wrong last year, it would be tempting for commentators to carry along in the same merry way, grandly predicting outcomes of elections and referendums on the basis of hunches and conversations with taxi drivers at party conferences (a favourite of lobby journalists keen to gauge the mood on the street without actually having to go onto the street itself). There seems to be little consequence to getting a general election wrong, and laughing off a backbencher standing for the Labour leadership as a bit of a joke, other than giving politicians something to mock us for.

But what *Sex, Lies and the Ballot Box* – and this, its sequel – has done is give us even less of an excuse to base our views of voters, party members and elections on our own half-baked theories and anecdotes.

After the first book, we were no longer left guessing as to the sexual preferences of the average Tory, or indeed whether voters just plump for the candidate they fancy. Groups of voters who politicians know they need to target but often end up patronising or generalising about are studied in this volume in serious detail, not sketched out in an arty fashion.

Politics can be a science, but so often it is treated as an art. It's not just journalists who get away with this: political 'gurus' earn far bigger bucks than we can ever dream of for handing parties their expertise based on campaigns in different countries featuring entirely different candidates. And if they fail, they tend to recover by saying they'd warned the candidate in question that they weren't going to win anyway, and move on to another campaign. But at least now, none of us have an excuse. This term, we really do need to read the book.

Introduction

Philip Cowley and Robert Ford

H ere is what is supposed to happen when you try to get academics involved in a project for non-academic consumption.

First, no one will be interested: all too insular, too busy, too much academic writing to do. Why communicate with the wider world when they can write for obscure journals read by three people and a dog?

Second, even those who are interested won't be up to the task. Dulled by decades of writing in academese for niche journals where being 'accessible' is a criticism, they lack the tools, the language, the tone to write for a broader audience.

And third, being academics, they won't deliver copy on time, so the book will arrive years late, or not at all.

All in all, wiser heads will argue, it is not worth putting yourselves through such an ordeal.

But we did anyway. And that wasn't our experience. When we pitched the idea of a book called *Sex, Lies and the Ballot Box* – the precursor to this volume – to our colleagues back in 2013, we found we had more volunteers than we had space for chapters.*

---

* If we're being completely accurate, when we originally pitched the idea the book's working title was *73% of Lib Dem Voters Eat Hummus*. We changed this for two reasons. First, because it's a rubbish title. And second, because it wasn't true. In 2011 YouGov found that just 38 per cent of Lib Dems liked hummus, with no significant difference between

We laid down clear ground rules. Each chapter must be just 1,000 words long. No jargon. Only one table or graph, only if really needed, and only if a layperson could understand it. And no footnotes. When we explained this last rule one colleague did a good impression of a robot from an early sci-fi film:

Does Not Compute.

Does Not Compute.

Head Explodes.

Sure, we had to exercise a firm editorial hand. Several people just ignored the rules, as academics are wont to do, and sent in drafts with multiple footnotes anyway. But the delete button is a wonderful thing.[†]

Writing for a wider audience can be tough, but who raises their kids to avoid challenges? There's an episode of *The Simpsons* in which Homer says, 'If something is too hard to do, then it's not worth doing.' Homer shouldn't be our role model. As for academics and deadlines, we'd asked for first drafts by 1 February. The last arrived on 19 July. By academic standards, that's almost ahead of schedule.

We soon realised that, far from being incapable of writing in the correct voice, most of our contributors were well versed in writing for non-academic audiences. They already ran websites, or wrote for blogs, or for newspapers, or otherwise contributed to policy debates. In the book's foreword, Danny Finkelstein of *The Times* claimed that the way political scientists engaged with the world outside academia was undergoing a revolution. We were, he said, 'forcing [our] data and conclusions on those who shouldn't be allowed simply to ignore them'. In its own modest way, that was the aim of the first book – as it is of this one.

Lib Dem voters and those of other parties. But if you looked at how those same people had voted in the election a year before, then 43 per cent of 2010 Lib Dems had been into hummus, with the Lib Dems the most pro-hummus party. One effect of coalition therefore had been to drive hummus eaters away from the Lib Dems.

† You will notice we do not obey this rule in the introduction. Our mantra: do as we say, not as we do.

There are still academics who are sniffy about engaging with the world. Their work, so they say, is just too sophisticated, too complicated, too *subtle* to disseminate to a wider audience. They operate at a higher level. Very occasionally this might be true, but it's usually self-justifying cobblers masking tedious content written by lazy authors. And the good news is that these academics tend to be older and will soon be dead.

But perhaps the most significant problem with the viewpoint of such fusty colleagues is that it fails to do justice to the audience outside the ivory tower. The book's reception proved there was a tremendous public appetite for clearly argued and carefully conducted research about elections and voters. Curiosity, after all, is a universal human quality. One of the great things about being a researcher is the freedom to indulge it. Why not bring others along for the ride?

It wasn't universally loved, though. One chapter reported on the sex lives of the different political tribes, and noted the relatively unimaginative and below par performance of UKIP voters. This prompted one woman to write to us to say that she was going to vote UKIP and she and her husband had a great sex life, so the research was clearly wrong. Well, perhaps. But maybe she was an outlier? Or maybe he was a secret Lib Dem? After all, the same research showed they were *filthy*.

Another review argued that the book was not so much full of conversation starters but conversation stoppers. When we reported this back to our contributors, they did not take it as a criticism. 'We are', one said, with a little too much enthusiasm, 'the sort of people who like to say: "it's a bit more complicated than that".'

And another review argued that the chapters on sex and politics were only included to attract headlines and generate publicity for the book. To which all we can say is that we seem to live in a depressingly cynical world.

Anyway, the success of that book persuaded Biteback to ask us for a second, and here it is. This isn't a second edition or a revised edition. It's a new book. All the chapters in this book are original, covering material not discussed in the first. A majority of the contributors are new as well, and as with the original book, we've tried to include a range of authors from rising stars to old farts. But the goals are the same: to try to explain elections and voting in an accessible way to as wide an audience as possible.

The chapters are all written by members of the Political Studies Association's specialist group on Elections, Public Opinion and Parties, known as EPOP, which has been running for over twenty years and is one of the PSA's most active groups. The book therefore is written by people who love elections, and for whom the electoral cycle is part of the natural rhythm of their lives. They look forward to the year's elections with the same enthusiasm that normal people await Christmas. Indeed, for many of our writers elections are as exciting as Christmas is for the *children* of normal people – and if you were wondering who Santa votes for, you can find out in Chapter 39.

We know from feedback that many of the first book's readers were indeed people who get unnaturally excited by polls and swingometers. But this book, like the first one, is also written for another audience: those who don't find elections as fascinating as we do, some of whom may even entertain the heretical thought that elections are a bit, well, dull.

We think they're wrong, and we want to show them why. People sometimes make the mistake of trying to justify the study of elections and voting on the basis that they are an important part of democracy, which they are – but things can be important without being interesting. Elections are important *and* interesting. At root, elections are interesting because they involve people – candidates, activists, voters, non-voters – and like most things involving people, explaining what they do and why they do it is not always straightforward. Sometimes it is depressing, sometimes it is uplifting, but always it is revealing. 'If we would learn what the human race really is at bottom,' wrote Mark Twain, 'we need only observe it at election time.' Not a lot has changed since Twain wrote that in 1885, except that the more we learn about elections, the more we realise how right he was.

The ideal voter of democratic theory is supposed to be a rational man or woman, someone who gathers all the evidence about the issues of the day and the plans of the parties, weighs it all up responsibly, cogitating at length, and then delivers a mature and informed judgement at the ballot box. Actual voters aren't much like that – which is why they are so interesting. In practice, voters' choices reflect the whole rich tapestry of human nature: swayed by emotions as well as reason, salesmen as well as products, by tribal attachment as well as cool calculation. To take a few examples from the following pages: voters respond to negative campaigning (though they claim to hate it), the race of their candidates (though they claim it doesn't bother them) and the church they are notionally attached to (though few ever go). What is more, their willingness to show up at all ebbs and flows with the seasons: voters, like bears, go into hibernation in the winter, as discussed in Chapter 9.

Most of this book focuses on Britain. In part that reflects the skew of interests in a British political science group. But it's also that Britain offers a particularly interesting case study for election researchers. We have an increasingly large number of elections – with an electoral cycle that now coughs up an important set of contests on a yearly basis – which use an increasingly eclectic set of electoral procedures.[‡]

---

‡ For example, elections for Westminster use one electoral system, the same as local elections in England and Wales. But local elections in Scotland use a different system, the same that is used in Northern Ireland for the European Parliament, although elections for the European Parliament in England, Wales and Scotland use another system altogether. And the elections for the Scottish Parliament and Welsh Assembly use a different system to that again, one which is similar to the one used for the London Assembly. But anyone voting for

Then there's the increasing use of referendums – with two UK-wide contests in the last decade alone, plus separate ones in Scotland, Wales and Northern Ireland. No one thinks those we've just seen will be the last, either.

Added to that, there are the voters, who are becoming ever more unpredictable, and continue to surprise even seasoned election watchers. Just since the last book came out in 2014 we have had, in no particular order: the Conservative majority victory in 2015 (something almost all observers and the polls said was impossible); the collapse of the Liberal Democrats, who fell to just eight seats, undoing at least a generation's work building the third force in British politics; the rise, but ultimately still the failure, of the United Kingdom Independence Party, who piled up almost four million votes, the best result for an 'other' party in modern British politics, but who achieved a paltry single Westminster seat as a reward; and, perhaps most spectacularly of all, the historic surge in support for the Scottish National Party, who took fifty-six of the fifty-nine seats in Scotland, destroying the Scottish Labour Party in the process, in what is probably the most significant change in the British party system since the formation of the Labour Party – and one of the largest swings in vote behaviour in one election cycle ever seen anywhere. (The paradox of the last of these is that on election night itself it was not all that surprising, but just a year before it would have seemed unimaginable.) Then, as we were editing chapters in spring 2016 we had the Scottish parliament elections in which Labour fell to third behind the Conservatives. In June, as we checked the book's proofs, we had the astonishing EU referendum campaign. When we received the proofs, David Cameron, Jeremy Corbyn and British EU membership were all seen as relatively

---

the London mayor – and mayoralty elections elsewhere – uses yet another system, which is the same as the one used in the elections for the police and crime commissioners. Confused? You wouldn't be the only one. It's bonkers. But it makes life fun (for us, at least).

secure. After we dispatched the final corrections, all three were gone or in doubt.

At times, the various referendum campaigns – especially the divided, divisive and feud-prone Out campaign (or campaigns) – appeared to be a complicated and sophisticated natural experiment set up by devious political scientists solely to test whether competent campaigns make much of a difference. The same could perhaps be said of the Labour leadership since 2015, a contest which delivered a leader few academics (or political punters) expected to win, and whose approach to elections and leadership flies in the face of the received wisdom of researchers and pundits alike. Whatever else you think about all of this, you can't say it's not interesting.

Then there's the data. The British Election Study – on which many of these chapters draw – has now been running continuously since the election of 1964, making it the longest-running electoral study in Europe and allowing us to quantify and analyse the ups and downs of mass politics over a sweep of more than fifty years, and there are now also far more 'normal' opinion polls than ever before, as the arrival of internet polling has pushed down the costs of data collection.

The polling debacle of 2015 – which is discussed in the opening chapter – has rather shaken faith in opinion polls. One of the many ironies of the 2015 general election in Britain was that those who knew next to nothing about the polls – or who chose to ignore them – were more likely to accurately predict the outcome than those who followed them closely. The result was that the pollsters spent much of the next year furiously analysing what went wrong. Yet for all the horror of 2015, polling still matters. Despite its flaws and limitations, polling is still (usually) better than the alternative – which is to make it up or to assume that you or your friends have some profound insight into the general population (you don't, they don't, none of us does). During the EU referendum campaign, it was common to hear people say how the polls must be wrong, because all of their friends were voting the same way as them; in a referendum that split the nation basically down the middle, this says more about them and their friends than about the opinion polls.

It is noticeable that the polling companies then did much better at subsequent contests, including the Labour leadership contest and the elections in Scotland, Wales and London. They were again criticised after the EU referendum – though on this occasion they delivered a split verdict, with some pointing to a Brexit vote, and (as discussed in Chapter 14) they did better than the betting markets. Besides, for all the scorn poured on the polls after 2015 by many Tories, it is noticeable that the victorious Conservatives privately spent a fortune on private polling in marginal seats, designed to track the effectiveness of their campaign and used to target resources. The answer to poor polling is not no polling but better polling. Ignorance, as Barack Obama said recently, is never a virtue; it's just not knowing stuff.

Like its predecessor, this isn't meant to be an introductory textbook. Rather, this volume offers an eclectic series of sketches, each introducing an aspect of elections and political behaviour. Each of the chapters offers a 1,000-word essay. These are not monographs, and many summarise years, in some cases decades, of research. Each chapter ends with a short account of further reading and there is a detailed bibliography in case any of the subject matter stirs you to dig deeper. We make no claim for comprehensiveness, but between them the following fifty chapters cover: polling, particularly the disaster of 2015, political geography, gender, sex, race, money, Scotland, candidates, partisanship, Wales, young people, trust, apathy, alienation, volatility, religion, issue ownership and salience, manifestos, party members and supporters, candidates, and class. We've deliberately expanded our scope to beyond these shores, and also include some vignettes on elections and politics from France, Switzerland, Germany, Japan, America, Ireland, Poland and Belgium.

Some examples from what follows: why campaigns don't matter very much; why you should forget about Mondeo Man; why the polls were so wrong and why the betting markets aren't always better than the polls; why (if you're a Labour voter) you should kiss a Tory; why men are more male than women are female; why dead voters are a growing problem; why politicians usually do what they say they will do, although much of what they say they will do is so vague that we will never know if they did it or not; why women don't vote for women (except for the few who do); how people want the freedom to be identical; why we're all (political) swingers now; how the weather affects your turnout; why negativity is positive; how the internet does not encourage voting (except when it does); why the National Trust is good for political engagement; and why – with apologies to Alastair Campbell – we do 'do God', after all. Plus, Santa. And there's a bonus 51st chapter on why being right-wing means you (probably) have a better sex life – indeed, a better life overall. We have not – categorically not – included this last chapter to generate press coverage for the book. Perish the thought.

Once again, our colleagues were enthusiastic about the project and a delight to work with. Editing a book like this was not always straightforward, but they have made it easier by always responding to our often detailed and insistent editorial requests swiftly and in good spirit. Well, almost always. We are also grateful to all the staff at Biteback for their fantastic support. We think the end result is worth it. We hope you do, too.

List of contributors

NICHOLAS ALLEN is Reader in Politics at Royal Holloway, University of London.

LYNN BENNIE is Reader in Politics at the University of Aberdeen.

GALINA BORISYUK is Lecturer in Advanced Statistical Methods at Plymouth University.

SHAUN BOWLER is Professor of Political Science at the University of California, Riverside.

TINA BURRETT is Associate Professor of Political Science at Sophia University, Japan.

ROSIE CAMPBELL is Professor of Politics at Birkbeck, University of London.

HAROLD CLARKE is Ashbel Smith Professor at the University of Texas at Dallas.

PHILIP COWLEY is Professor of Politics at Queen Mary University of London.

DAVID CUTTS is Reader in Political Science at the University of Bath.

JAMES DENNISON is a Researcher in the Social and Political Science Department of the European University Institute, Florence.

GEOFFREY EVANS is Professor of Politics and Fellow of Nuffield College, Oxford.

JOCELYN EVANS is Professor of Politics at the University of Leeds.

JUSTIN FISHER is Professor of Political Science at Brunel University London.

STEPHEN D. FISHER is Associate Professor in Political Sociology, and Fellow and tutor in Politics at Trinity College, University of Oxford.

ROBERT FORD is Professor of Political Science at the University of Manchester.

STUART FOX is a Quantitative Research Associate in the Wales Institute for Social Research, Data and Methods at Cardiff University.

CHRIS GAME is Honorary Senior Lecturer at the University of Birmingham's Institute of Local Government Studies (INLOGOV).

MATTHEW GOODWIN is Professor of Politics at the University of Kent.

JANE GREEN is Professor of Political Science at the University of Manchester.

OLIVER HEATH is Reader in Politics at Royal Holloway, University of London.

AILSA HENDERSON is Professor of Political Science at the University of Edinburgh.

DAN HOUGH is Professor of Politics at the University of Sussex.

WILL JENNINGS is Professor of Political Science and Public Policy at the University of Southampton.

ROB JOHNS is Reader in Politics at the University of Essex.

RON JOHNSTON is Professor in the School of Geographical Sciences at the University of Bristol.

MICHAEL MARSH is Emeritus Professor of Political Science at Trinity College Dublin.

NICOLE MARTIN is a Senior Research Officer at the University of Essex.

LAUREN MCLAREN is Professor of Comparative Politics at the University of Glasgow.

JONATHAN MELLON is a Research Fellow at Nuffield College, Oxford.

CAITLIN MILAZZO is Associate Professor at the University of Nottingham.

JAMES MORRIS is a Partner at Greenberg Quinlan Rosner.

MARK PACK is co-author of the Liberal Democrat agents' handbook and Associate Director at communications agency Blue Rubicon.

SAM POWER is a PhD student and Associate Tutor at the University of Sussex.

CHRISTOPHER PROSSER is a Research Associate at the University of Manchester.

KINGSLEY PURDAM is a Senior Lecturer in the School of Social Sciences at the University of Manchester.

COLIN RALLINGS is Professor of Politics at Plymouth University and Co-Director of the Elections Centre.

RICHARD ROSE is Professor and Director of the Centre for the Study of Public Policy at the University of Strathclyde Glasgow.

JAVIER SAJURIA is a Research Associate in the School of Government and Public Policy, University of Strathclyde Glasgow.

LUKAS SCHMID is Assistant Professor at the University of Lucerne.

ROGER SCULLY is Professor of Political Science in the Wales Governance Centre at Cardiff University.

BEN SEYD is a Lecturer in Politics at the University of Kent.

MATT SINGH runs Number Cruncher Politics, the polling and elections website.

MARIA SOBOLEWSKA is a Senior Lecturer in Politics at the University of Manchester.

BEN STANLEY is a Lecturer at SWPS University, Warsaw.

CHRIS TERRY is a Researcher at the Electoral Reform Society.

MICHAEL THRASHER is Professor of Politics at Plymouth University and Co-Director of the Elections Centre.

JAMES TILLEY is Professor of Politics at the University of Oxford and a Fellow of Jesus College, Oxford.

JOE TWYMAN is Head of Political and Social Research at YouGov.

MATT WALL is a Senior Lecturer in Politics at Swansea University's Department of Political and Cultural Studies.

NICOLA WILDASH is a Research Executive in the Political team at YouGov.

CHRISTOPHER WLEZIEN is Hogg Professor of Government at the University of Texas at Austin.

'In God we trust, all others bring data.'

ATTRIBUTED TO W. EDWARDS DEMING (ALTHOUGH THERE IS, IRONICALLY, NO DATA TO SUGGEST HE SAID IT)

CHAPTER 1

The failure of a generation:
the polling debacle of 2015

Matt Singh

Since the 2015 general election, one polling question has come up again and again – how did the polls get it so disastrously wrong? Opinion polls at the election underestimated the Conservative lead over Labour by 6.5 points. This was similar to the error seen in 1970 and almost as serious as the 9-point miss in 1992.

In the time since, a lot of work has been done on the subject, all of which arrives at similar conclusions. There is little sign that voters changed their minds at the last minute, or that people who told pollsters they would vote Labour ended up staying home. Some people may have given contradictory answers to pollsters, but even if they actually lied there were far too few of them to be the main cause of the problem. Rather, in simple terms, pollsters' samples weren't representative of the country – they contained too many Labour voters and not enough Conservatives. During the campaign, pollsters spoke to a total of 15,291 Conservative voters compared to 15,368 Labour voters.

Getting a representative sample of the population has become more difficult over time, but steadily rather than suddenly, and pollsters have worked hard to correct for it. Likewise, some parties' voters are more likely to show up and vote than others, but this too is a long-standing problem. So why did the polls suddenly go off balance in 2015?

One problem is interest: people who are willing to answer polls on politics tend to have atypically high levels of interest in politics. As the figure shows, 9 per cent of British people rated their own attention to politics as 9/10 or 10/10 in the British Election Study (BES), which conducted a high-quality face-to-face survey over several months after the election. But nearly a quarter of those sampled by opinion polls before the election were from this super-attentive group.

RESPONDENTS' ATTENTION TO POLITICS IN PRE-ELECTION POLLS AND THE BRITISH ELECTION STUDY

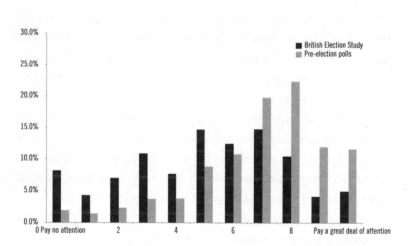

That's a big enough problem on its own. But what made it worse was that this political engagement problem was unevenly spread across different types of voters. There was a particular segment of the electorate that was consistently under-sampled in polls – people who aren't hugely engrossed in politics, who might not vote in a council or European election, but who *do* vote in general elections. In both 2010 and 2015, this type of person voted Conservative by some margin.

But there was one last line of defence that ought to have saved the pollsters. Since 1992, the last major polling debacle in Britain, polling companies have paid close attention to the *political* makeup of their samples, rather than simply the demographics. At its most basic, this involves asking people how they voted in the last general election, and comparing their answers to the results.

This partisan weighting, which normally helps to ensure samples are reasonably representative, simply wasn't able to cope with the complicated flows of voters from one party to another this time around. The polls had the right proportions of each party's 2010 voters, but not of their 2015 voters. The polls ultimately got it wrong because the flows of voters switching between the parties, in a parliament that saw the Lib Dems collapse and UKIP surge, were completely at odds with what the polls had shown. The pollsters' results found people who voted Lib Dem in 2010 were switching disproportionately to Labour and much less to the Conservatives. Meanwhile, UKIP's rise was hurting the Tories more than Labour. This intuitively all made sense – one half of the Lib Dems' family tree (the Social Democratic Party) was founded by moderates who quit Labour in the early 1980s, while UKIP was founded by ex-Tory Eurosceptics.

But the picture emerging from the actual election results and the more comprehensive post-election BES survey was very different. It turns out that in the last parliament, both the Conservatives and Labour gained votes in almost equal measure from the Lib Dems, while losing them in almost equal measure to UKIP. Labour did gain more than the Tories from Lib Dem switching, but only narrowly. The polls also consistently underestimated the threat to Labour from UKIP. On average, they were right about the overall level of UKIP support, but wrong about where it came from. They had typically shown at least two and as many as three 2010 Conservative voters defecting to UKIP for each 2010 Labour voter switching. But the election results and the post-election BES data both suggest it was far more even than this.

And since many of the UKIP supporters that voted Conservative in 2010 were Labour voters in elections before that, in all likelihood UKIP has taken more voters from Labour over the last decade than from the Conservatives. The idea of a split on the right and a reunification on the left was wrong; the 'revolt on the right' hurt the centre-left just as much.

Polls had also suggested that very few voters were moving directly between Labour and the Conservatives, and those that did cancelled each other out. But actually there was a slight net impact, and in the Tories' favour. The Conservatives managed to gain support from former Labour voters, something the pollsters largely missed.

These errors also help explain why the Scottish and London polls in 2015 were much nearer the mark than those of the whole of Great Britain. London was UKIP's weakest region anywhere in England and Wales, while 2010 Lib Dem voters in the capital actually did mostly go to Labour, even if they behaved differently elsewhere. In Scotland, UKIP made very little impact, while the ex-Lib Dems were mostly swallowed by the SNP.

So the polls got it wrong, not for a single reason, but from a deadly cocktail of risks. The samples were unrepresentative, but crucially the demographic weighting techniques used to correct this were ineffective, and the political weightings developed after the last polling failure were unable to cope with the much higher electoral flux between 2010 and 2015. Had any of these three problems not arisen, disaster might well have been averted. But in combination, they resulted in the polling failure of a generation.

FURTHER READING

For the official report of the British Polling Council, see *Report of the Inquiry into the 2015 British General Election Opinion Polls* by Patrick Sturgis et al. (Market Research Society and British Polling Council, 2016). For further detail on the causes of the polling failure, see 'Missing Non-Voters and Misweighted Samples: Explaining the 2015 Great British Polling Miss', by Jon Mellon and Chris Prosser on the British Election Study blog (2015), or 'Where the polls went wrong' on the Number Cruncher Politics blog (2015). For the pre-election analysis that predicted the disaster and Conservative victory, see 'Is there a shy Tory factor in 2015?', also on the Number Cruncher Politics blog (2015).

'It is the folly of too many to mistake the echo of a London coffee-house for the voice of the kingdom.'

JONATHAN SWIFT

— CHAPTER 2 —

Mondeo meh: the myth of target voters

James Morris

In the run up to every election, newspapers fill with articles about the handful of voters that will supposedly swing the result – soccer moms, NASCAR dads, Worcester women, pebbledash families. Occasionally this analysis is useful. Normally it is not. In the last five UK elections, 90 per cent of demographic groups swung in the same way as the population as a whole.

A common trick to make a target group sound exciting is to focus on what is distinctive about a group, at the expense of what is important about them. For example, *Guardian* readers are more likely to be Labour voters (60 per cent voted Labour in 2015) than *Mail* readers (20 per cent). But the *Mail* sells nine times as many copies as the *Guardian*, more than enough to compensate for the difference. If you want to target Labour voters, the *Mail* reaches more of them than the *Guardian*.

Another technique is to present polling results comparing one subgroup with another, without mentioning specific numbers. It allows you to say things like 'older men were twice as likely as younger women to think the Conservatives are on the side of ordinary people'.

This sounds significant until you realise that the numbers in question (from a poll I carried out for the TUC) are 6 per cent and 3 per cent.

So why do we get all this fuss about Mondeo Man and his friends whenever an election rolls around?

It is partly because establishing the importance of particular groups can be politically useful. Campaigning organisations have a particular interest in arguing that their client group will be decisive and therefore make hyperbolic claims about the group's electoral influence to attract attention from the parties and the press.

Take as an example the claim from Operation Black Vote that 'the black vote can decide the 2015 general election'. This was based on analysis which found 168 seats where ethnic minority voters outnumbered the majority of the sitting MP. Operation Black Vote is a great organisation that has achieved a lot, but this argument for electoral significance is equally true of every demographic group in those seats which was at least as populous as ethnic minority communities. It would apply to women, men, the over-forties, the under-forties, mums, dads, grandparents, racists, anti-racists, believers in astrology, pet-owners and so on. It isn't possible for all those groups to be decisive.

Thinking of electoral targets in terms of demographic niches leads parties to develop policies aimed at each niche. This is exactly the effect that lobbyists want, but it is far from a ticket to electoral success. As Labour found in 2015, firing popular rent cap policies at young people in Harlow and popular energy policies at older people in Cleethorpes made no difference when Labour wasn't able to boost trust on the fundamentals of leadership and economic credibility. Lots of hyper-targeted policy, even if it is very popular with the target audiences, is not enough to secure victory.

Parties that successfully use targeting use it in three ways.

First, they use geographic targets: marginal seats, swing districts and battleground states. This form of targeting is absolutely fundamental to campaign design in constituency-focused political systems. Resources are poured into districts where an extra pound might make a difference, and kept out of places where a party is confident of victory or defeat.

Second, their micro-targeted appeals curate and tailor the overall message, but they do not try to create a separate message. The 2016 Democratic primary was a great example of this. Bernie Sanders's strength with young people did not come through specific youth-oriented policy offers, but because his overall message attacking corporate greed and calling for radical change resonated particularly strongly with young people. Similarly, Hillary Clinton's success hinged on African-American and Latino voters, and came as a result of her broadcast messaging and the lasting popularity of the Clinton brand with these groups. Individualised messages on Facebook and other digital platforms fit within these overall frameworks and amplify the most compelling elements for individuals.

Third, parties use targeting as a form of internal communications. This is partly about projecting sophistication by showing that campaign chiefs are super-advanced political strategists who can say 'big data' a lot. More importantly, it is about directing resources and explaining to party members and volunteers that the people they are trying to persuade have different priorities and values to your typical activist.

One of the most famous target groups in British politics was Mondeo Man. According to Tony Blair: 'His dad voted Labour. He used to vote Labour, too. But he'd bought his own house now. He'd set up his own business. He was doing very nicely. His instincts were to get on in life.' Parse that: he's a man (49 per cent of the population); from a family where at least one parent voted Labour (back when 90 per cent voted either Labour or Conservative); owns his own home (65 per cent of the population); self-employed (so could be in the trades, or running a shop or a small company), and his instincts tell him to work hard and succeed (almost everyone). In short, Mondeo Man was a pretty normal kind of a guy in the types of marginal seat Labour was trying to win. It says less about New Labour's psephological genius and more about the peculiar internal politics of the party that this kind of person was a stretching target.

FURTHER READING

For more on how data-driven targeted campaigning can shift the vote see *The Victory Lab* (Broadway Books, 2012) by Sasha Issenberg. For a more sceptical take, have a look at *The Gamble* (Princeton University Press, 2014) by John Sides and Lynn Vavreck. Justin Fisher's paper 'Constituency Campaigning at the 2015 General Election' looks at local campaign effects, while the co-editor of this volume has a tome, *The British General Election of 2015* (Palgrave Macmillan, 2016), that gives an insight into what the parties themselves think decided the campaign. For a look at how big picture social and demographic changes shape elections more than campaign activity read *America Ascendant* (Thomas Dunne Books, 2015) by Stan Greenberg.

—CHAPTER 3—

The (mostly) pre-baked cake: polls and votes

Christopher Wlezien

Even when elections aren't in the offing, we are awash with opinion polls tapping vote intentions. During the heat of campaigns, rarely a day passes without the release of a new poll, often multiple polls on the same day. What do they tell us about the final outcome?

Despite all of the problems with polling in 2015 (as discussed in Chapter 1), surveys of vote intentions taken just before voters cast their ballots have done well anticipating the outcome of elections. Of course, there are exceptions, but for the most part – in the UK and other countries – polls immediately before the election are fairly accurate.

What about earlier? One way to test this is to compare the vote, say, for every British election for which we have polls, with poll results from the day before the election, two days before, three days before, and so on, as far back as we have data available. (For days with missing polls, we can interpolate based on polls on surrounding dates.) We then can see how the actual vote lines up with the polls day by day.

When we do this, we observe three main patterns. First, there are a lot more polls late in the election cycle than there are earlier, which is as one would expect. Second, the spread of poll-vote errors shrinks using later and later polls, which also is as one would expect. Third, preferences come into focus steadily over the long campaign; taking all British elections since 1945, the average poll error drops from 6.6 per cent two years before elections to 4.1 per cent a year out, and it declines further still to 3.3 per cent before the final month of the campaign and then to 2.1 per cent at the very end. The late 'official' campaign still does have a small effect on preferences but the biggest changes occur more than a year in advance. In other words, the electoral cake is substantially baked well before voters go to the polls.

ERRORS IN VOTE INTENTION POLLS FOR PRESIDENTIAL AND PARLIAMENTARY ELECTIONS, BY MONTH BEFORE THE ELECTION, FOR FORTY-FIVE COUNTRIES BETWEEN 1945 AND 2010

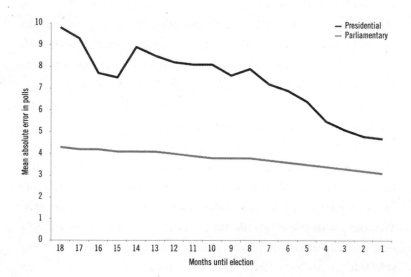

The pattern we observe in the UK is strikingly general, in that it broadly holds across a wide range of countries with very different political institutions. That said, there are differences, and electoral institutions and government institutions do matter. The most pronounced difference is between presidential elections on the one hand and parliamentary elections on the other.

This can be seen in the figure, which depicts the average errors of poll shares at different points in the election cycle for all major parties – with vote shares greater than 5 per cent – for the two types of elections. There are forty-five countries included in the analysis, twenty-three of which hold presidential elections and twenty-eight of which hold parliamentary elections. The number of presidential and parliamentary elections exceeds the total number of countries (forty-five) used in the analysis because some countries with 'semi-presidential' systems (like France) have both types of elections.

The figure draws on 26,000 opinion polls, and plots the monthly mean absolute error (MAE) in the polls, calculated separately for presidential and parliamentary elections, for all elections between 1945 and 2010. The x-axis depicts the number of months before election day, starting eighteen months in advance, and the y-axis the MAE of the polls, where high values indicate that the average difference between poll results and the vote is large.

In both sets of elections, the average error declines, which means that polls become more informative the closer the election. As discussed above, this comes as little surprise, but it nevertheless makes clear that preferences evolve over time. What may surprise is that the decline is fairly linear, particularly for parliamentary elections. This means that preferences evolve steadily, not in an episodic way. We can see that the decline is much greater for presidential elections, however. There, early polls are not at all informative about the vote – with errors more than double those in parliamentary systems eighteen months before elections – and the outcome comes into increasing focus over time, particularly the year before the election. In parliamentary elections, by contrast, poll readings from well in advance tell us a great deal about the final outcome, perhaps even more than those from the final month in presidential elections.

The patterns shed light on the evolution of electoral preferences in different countries – specifically, that preferences develop earlier in parliamentary systems. This reflects fundamental differences between the systems. Whereas in presidential elections voters select an individual to represent the country, in parliamentary elections they select a legislature, which in turn produces a government. Understandably, parties tend to matter more in the latter than the former, which is important, as dispositions toward parties, while not constant, are fairly durable. They are thus to a large extent in place early. In presidential elections, by contrast, candidates often are not even known until the election year, as in the 2016 US presidential race. Even where presidential candidates are known earlier, full information about their characteristics and positions is not; it becomes clear as the election year unfolds. In short, voters' preferences crystallise earlier in parliamentary systems than in presidential ones because the information voters use to decide is available earlier.

Other factors influence the match between polls and the vote, if to a lesser extent. Most notably, research shows that polls are more informative in party-centric parliamentary systems, which fits nicely with the reasoning above. That these systems tend to be associated with proportional electoral rules implies that these electoral rules also matter, if only indirectly. There also is reason to think that characteristics of the parties themselves are important, especially their size and age. When the frenzy of the next election campaign gets under way, it is worth remembering that the stakes are often lower than they appear. By the time politicians hit the doorsteps, most of the electoral race has already been run.

FURTHER READING

The original study of daily polls and the vote in US presidential elections appeared in 'The Timeline of Presidential Election Campaigns' (*Journal of Politics*, 2002), with the analysis extended in Robert S. Erikson and Christopher Wlezien's *The Timeline of Presidential Elections: How Campaigns Do (and Do Not) Matter* (University of Chicago Press, 2012). Wlezien et al. analysed British elections in 'Polls and the Vote in Britain' (*Political Studies*, 2013) and Jennings and Wlezien recently published an analysis of forty-five countries, entitled 'The Timeline of Elections: A Comparative Perspective' (*American Journal of Political Science*, 2016).

—CHAPTER 4—

Turn over, tune out and log off: the irrelevance of campaigns

Mark Pack

Think back to the last time you saw an Olympics medal ceremony. Did you wait with bated breath to see who would outpace the others and snatch the gold by beating them to the top step? Of course not. Because we all know who gets which medal has been determined before the medal ceremony. A commentator who narrated the walk out to the podium as if it determines who gets the gold medal would, rightly, be dismissed as eccentric. Possibly lovable, but certainly eccentric.

Yet when it comes to British general elections nearly everyone falls foul of the same eccentric behaviour, treating the last few weeks of a parliamentary cycle – the formal general election campaign – as if they are what determines the election result. But as the previous chapter has shown, much of the race has been run long before the formal campaign – and in almost every general election in the last sixty years the party that was ahead in the polls months before the formal election campaign started was the one that went on to win.

The rush of extended political coverage in newspapers, the special extra TV broadcasts, the journalists sent on tours of marginal seats in 'quirky' forms of transport, the extra generosity of financial donors, the ramping up of political party advertising campaigns, the prognostications of pundits about how today's events might be the turning point in the campaign – they are all far too late. The result is already settled.

The table below gives you the data to prove it. It lists each general election since 1955, showing the party ahead in the polls in January of that year – and then the winning party when the votes were counted.

PARTIES AHEAD AT START OF YEAR AND AT GENERAL ELECTION

ELECTION	PARTY AHEAD IN THE POLLS	PARTY WHICH GOT THE MOST VOTES
1964	Labour	Labour
1966	Labour	Labour
1970	Conservative	Conservative
1974 Feb	Conservative	Conservative (but Labour got most seats)
1974 Oct	n/a	Labour
1979	Conservative	Conservative
1983	Conservative	Conservative
1987	Conservative	Conservative
1992	Conservative	Conservative
1997	Labour	Labour
2001	Labour	Labour
2005	Labour	Labour
2010	Conservative	Conservative
2015	Labour	Conservative

Source: Data taken from the opinion poll database at http://www.markpack.org.uk/opinion-polls/.

Across these fourteen elections, in twelve cases the party ahead in January went on to win. The two exceptions are of the sort that really do fit the 'exception that proves the rule' cliché. One, in 2015, was a case when the opinion polls turned out to be way out (as discussed in Chapter 1). If you adjust polling figures from January 2015 in line with the polls' final errors then the rule still works (as it does if you make similar adjustments for the other two general elections where the polls were way out). The second exception is October 1974 where looking at the January figures is meaningless because going back to January means going back to before the *previous* general election. But even in the short interregnum between the two 1974 elections, the basic point that the party ahead well in advance went on to win still holds. Nor is January a magic month – the same strong overall pattern persists with a wrinkle or two along the way if you nudge the calendar a little this way or that.

So there you have an evidence-based approach to political punditry: take a look at the polls in January and then ignore them. Either they tell you who the winner is going to be, or they turn out to be so wrong that looking at them in later months would not be much help anyway.

Why is it the case that the sound and fury of election campaigns themselves make so little difference to who wins? Partly it is down to the campaign efforts of different parties mostly cancelling each other out. (If a political party would like to try out not campaigning at all so we can test this more rigorously, please do get in touch.) Partly it is due to the heavy influence of demography, class and habits on people's voting intentions, none of which change more than a smidgen during the brevity of an election campaign itself. Partly it is down to the influence of parties' reputations, which also come with years of baggage rather than being altered in the heat of the last few weeks of a campaign. Even when a single moment does shift a party's reputation – as with the Conservatives when Britain crashed out of the Exchange Rate Mechanism (ERM) in 1992 – these moments usually happen outside election campaigns because they are caused by events and decisions on a more fundamental scale than who said what at which press conference (or, these days, on Twitter).

So what should you do? Pay more attention to the past. If you wanted to understand the 2015 general election, you would have been far better off paying attention to how Labour failed to defend its economic record in 2010–11 than the latest twists of Ed Miliband's face as he came into contact with voters or bacon rolls.

Of course, in close individual seats the last few weeks of the campaign can certainly make a difference, and for those who are putting in the sort of campaigning hours each week that make junior doctors look like part-timers, what happens in the last few weeks of their years of effort in a seat certainly does matter to them. It can also make a difference to the margin of victory, influencing how the predicted winner ends up governing even if it does not change who the winner is.

But for the bigger picture as to who is going to win and the name of the next Prime Minister? Take a look at the polls shortly after Christmas time, place a bet if you are a betting person and put your feet up. You can safely let almost all the political news pass you by without altering your understanding of the likely election result and its causes. And if you do want to know why the result is going to be what it will be, turn off the rolling news, log out of Twitter and open a history book or two.

FURTHER READING

For an expert dissection of the impact of longer-term factors on voting behaviour over several recent British general elections, see *Affluence, Austerity and Electoral Change in Britain* (Oxford University Press, 2013) by Paul Whiteley et al. The Labour Party in particular has lost a sequence of general elections due to long-term factors, and a good picture of how such issues are seen through the eyes of voters is painted in Deborah Mattinson's *Talking to a Brick Wall* (Biteback, 2010). More broadly, there is evidence that campaigns can matter in lower-profile elections and in other countries. A good review of the research on this is in 'How Do Campaigns Matter?' by Gary C. Jacobson (*Annual Review of Political Science*, 2015).

'People never lie so much as after a hunt, during a war or before an election.'

ATTRIBUTED TO OTTO VON BISMARCK

— CHAPTER 5 —

We don't do God? Religion and vote choice in Britain

James Tilley

I n 2003 Alastair Campbell famously interrupted an interview with Tony Blair to tell the journalist that 'we don't do God'. That succinctly summarises the role of religion in elite political discourse in Britain over the last fifty years. Very few politicians refer to religion and very few, ironically with the exception of Tony Blair, are overtly religious. This is perhaps not surprising as Britain is a largely secular country and the role of religion in post-war politics has generally been perceived as weak. This perception is wrong.

In fact, religion has long been a good predictor of vote choices, and remains so today. If we look at survey data stretching back to the early 1980s, there are large and constant differences between different religious denominations in their party preferences. Moreover these are in the opposite direction to the differences that we see on the continent. In France, Poland or Spain, practising Catholics are much more likely to support parties of the right, whereas British Catholics vote for the left. As the figure below shows in England, the gap between Catholics and practising Anglicans in their support for Labour is a consistent 25 percentage points. In Scotland, this gap was even larger, with three quarters of Catholics regularly voting Labour prior to the party's collapse in 2015, compared to only a third of practising Presbyterians. Those with no religion, and non-conformists in England (not shown in the graph), lie somewhere between these two extremes. As an aside, the recent change for those with no religion in Scotland is due to the sharp rise of the SNP among that group, which predated the 2015 surge in SNP support more generally.

One obvious explanation might be that this is simply the disguised effects of class, or other social characteristics like age. If Catholics are more working-class than Anglicans then the explanation for Catholics voting Labour may be their class not their religion. This is not the case. Holding constant a large array of different social characteristics like class, income, education, region and so forth, differences in party choice by religious denomination remain. The other obvious explanation is that people in different denominations have different values, different policy attitudes and different national identities, and it is these which explain their vote choices. Again, this is not the case. Holding constant people's levels of social conservatism, economic leftism and national identity still does not reduce these religious differences.

An alternative explanation is that these voting patterns are a legacy of the religious divisions of the nineteenth and early twentieth centuries. Before the emergence of the Labour Party, when only a minority of men could cast their vote for the Liberals or Conservatives, religious denomination was important. The Liberals were clearly aligned with non-conformists in the nineteenth and early twentieth centuries. This was related not just to the disestablishment of Anglicanism in Wales, but also education policy and the temperance movement. Conversely, the Conservatives were seen as the party of the Church of England. The Church of England was the established church, and the Conservatives were the party of established privilege.

LABOUR SUPPORT BY RELIGION OVER TIME

England and Wales

Scotland

Note: The graphs show three-year moving averages of the proportion of people who identify with the Labour Party over time as a proportion of supporters of the main parties (three in England and Wales, along with the SNP in Scotland). Presbyterian refers to practising members of the Church of Scotland (those who attend church a few times a year or more) and Anglican refers to practising members of the Church of England (again, those who attend church a few times a year or more). Catholic refers to everyone who identifies themselves as Catholic regardless of religious practice. Data comes from the British Social Attitudes Surveys from 1983–2014.

These relationships were then complicated by the emergence of the Labour Party, which explicitly mobilised Catholics as the party grew in the early twentieth century. This was related to the issue of Irish home rule, which Labour supported, but also the fact that Catholics in Britain were predominantly working-class Irish immigrants who would naturally support the new workers' party. Denominations were linked to different parties in a particular way, and this is the pattern that remains today. Catholics, unlike in every other European country, are still more likely to support the British left today. Equally, non-conformists are still somewhat more likely to support the Liberals, and practising members of the established churches in both Scotland and England are more likely to support the establishment party of the Conservatives. The denominational patterns that we see today are the same patterns evident in the late nineteenth and early twentieth centuries.

Why do these differences persist? One crucial mechanism is inheritance. Religion maintains its link with party loyalties via parental socialisation into both a religious and party identity when children are growing up. People who are successful in passing on their religion to their children also tend to be successful in passing on their partisanship. Religious voting is thus a relic of past associations between groups and parties: religious divisions remain because religion is a marker of parents' and grandparents' party affiliation from an era when religion did matter for policy choices and for voters. These findings suggest that divisions that seem to be built on very little today can ironically be more resilient than those, like class, that seem to be built more firmly on the self-interest of today's voters.

Of course, there is a big caveat to all this. Fewer and fewer people are religious. In that sense, religion at the next election will play a smaller role than it did fifty years ago. Nonetheless, there is still a sizeable minority of people in Britain with a religious identity that matters for political choices (around a third of the electorate, depending on how it is measured) and the divisions between denominational groups are just as strong as they ever were. It is also the case that, while non-Christian religions make up only a small percentage of the population, they are growing in number and are very distinctive in their voting patterns. Somewhere between 4 and 5 per cent of the British electorate identify as Muslim, and three quarters of Muslims who voted in 2015 supported Labour. Much like Catholics a century ago, Muslim immigrants have been attracted to the Labour Party for reasons of policy (on immigration and race relations) and economics (Muslim immigrants tend to be poorer). It therefore seems reasonable to think that the trajectory of Muslim voters, remaining tied to the Labour Party, will be similar to Catholics. Either way, it is a safe prediction that religion will remain linked to vote choice in the future, even as the number of religious people continues gently to decline.

FURTHER READING

For the origins of political divisions based on religion in Britain, see Kenneth Wald's book *Crosses on the Ballot* (Princeton University Press, 1983). For more recent accounts of how religion continues to shape politics in Britain see 'We Don't Do God? Religion and Party Choice in Britain' by James Tilley (*British Journal of Political Science*, 2015) and *Religion and Public Opinion in Britain* by Ben Clements (Palgrave Macmillan, 2015). For more detail of how religion affects politics in European countries see the edited volume *Religion and Mass Electoral Behaviour in Europe* (Routledge, 2000) or *Sacred and Secular* by Pippa Norris and Ronald Inglehart (Cambridge University Press, 2004).

—CHAPTER 6—

All swingers now? The rise and rise of the British swing voter

Jonathan Mellon

F or decades political parties have competed furiously for one of the great prizes of British politics: the affections of the swing voter. It wasn't that long ago that there were relatively few political swingers: until the 1990s, fewer than a quarter of voters would switch parties from one election to the next.

Yet that once relatively rare breed is becoming increasingly common, which means party campaigners are going to have to come up with new tactical thinking. The British Election Study survey panels, conducted episodically over the last fifty years, are unique in that they are able to track the same voters from one election to the next, unlike more conventional opinion polls that only look at a snapshot of voters at a given time. Using these studies, you can identify the percentage of voters who switch their vote from one party to another between each pair of elections since 1966 when such data was first collected.

In 1966 only around 13 per cent of voters had changed their minds since the previous election in 1964. Since then, the proportion of swingers has been steadily increasing, and by 2015, 38 per cent of voters backed a different party to the one they supported in 2010.

The increase in swing voters is pretty consistent. The only exceptions are between February and October 1974, when (understandably) fewer voters changed their minds in eight months than switched in the preceding four years, and between 1997 and 2001, when the electoral dominance of New Labour under Tony Blair held back the tide for a time. These two exceptions aside, the increase has been constant election-on-election.

A lot of vote shifting can go on even between elections where the overall result remains stable. In 2001, for example, more people switched votes than in any election before 1997, with a surprising level of turmoil beneath the surface stability. While these largely cancelled out on that occasion, it set the stage for more dramatic changes in the parties' votes later on.

So British voters now seem more likely than ever to jump from party to party. But who exactly are these swingers? Are they disillusioned former party loyalists? Or have British voters simply stopped getting into a serious relationship with the parties in the first place? We can get some insight into this using data from the yearly British Social Attitudes Survey, looking at the number of respondents who say that they do not identify with any of the political parties (party identifiers tend to switch much less often) when they are asked 'Generally speaking, do you think of yourself as a supporter of any one political party?' and then 'Do you think of yourself as a little closer to one political party than to the others?' if they say no to the first question. The graph below combines data from 1984 to 2013. Each line represents people who were born in a different year. Higher lines mean that there are more people who do not identify with a political party. So, for instance, voters born in 1955 started with very low levels of non-identification (22 per cent), which have gradually risen to 44 per cent in the latest survey. Most of the lines on the graph go up over time, which shows that almost all generations are falling out of love with the parties.

However, an acquired taste in swinging among the older generations is dwarfed by the promiscuous younger generations – shown
by the dashed lines – most of whom never form an attachment to a
party at all. Each generation in the data has been less committed to
the parties than the previous generation was at the same age, with
around 60 per cent of the youngest generation – those born since
1985 – expressing no attachment to any political party.

PARTY IDENTIFICATION BY AGE COHORT

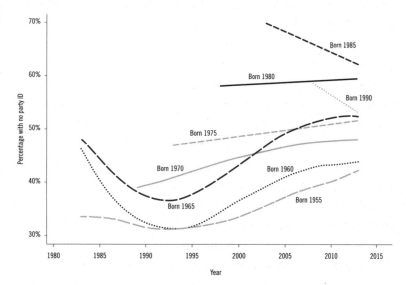

Since most of this change has been a generational shift, it may be a
long road back for the parties. Loyalty to parties is often handed down
in families, with children inheriting their parents' commitment to a
party. Now that this process has broken down, and younger generations have lost their attachment to parties, they may in turn pass on
this political detachment to their children.

The majority of younger voters have simply never grown up with the idea of getting into a long-term relationship with a political party, so they may never settle down. Many Labour MPs were outraged when it turned out that lots of the new members who joined up to vote for Jeremy Corbyn had voted for the Green Party just a few months before, but this may simply reflect the political approach of a generation who see parties as needing to earn their vote each time rather than commanding lasting, even unconditional loyalty.

If Britain's newfound taste for swinging isn't going to disappear any time soon, what does it mean for party competition? In the past most people had settled partisan views, which seldom changed. General elections could be won by attracting the relatively small group of voters who hadn't made up their minds and could very easily vote for either of the two main parties, so political parties based their strategies around mobilising their core voters and targeting the few waverers. While they worried about traditional loyalists not turning up to the polls, the parties could be assured of their supporters' votes as long as they got them to the voting booth.

Nowadays, swing voters are no longer a small section of the electorate who are being pulled back and forth by the parties, but a substantial chunk of all voters. This helps to explain why politicians have been so surprised by the sudden rise of new parties competing for groups previously thought to be reliable supporters. The new parties that have entered British politics have also allowed voters to express their views on issues that don't fall neatly into traditional left–right politics such as immigration (UKIP) or Scottish independence (the SNP). This in turn has posed a dilemma for the traditional parties, who are pulled in multiple directions trying to stop their voters being tempted away.

This may just be the start. If the number of swing voters stays this high, the parties will have to get used to defending themselves on multiple fronts.

FURTHER READING

For a slightly longer discussion of these recent trends see 'Party Attachment in Great Britain: Five Decades of Dealignment' by Jonathan Mellon (SSRN, 2016). Earlier work has also suggested several explanations for these British trends including *Decade of Dealignment* by Bo Särlvik and Ivor Crewe (Cambridge University Press, 1983), and 'The Dynamics of Party Identification Reconsidered' by Harold Clarke and Allan McCutcheon (*Public Opinion Quarterly*, 2009). Other work looks at trends across countries such as 'Party Identification and Party Choice' by Frode Berglund et al. in *The European Voter* (Oxford University Press, 2005) and 'Is the Party Over? The Decline of Party Activism and Membership across the Democratic World' by Paul Whiteley (*Party Politics*, 2011).

— CHAPTER 7 —

Racism at the ballot box: ethnic minority candidates

Stephen D. Fisher

Britain's ethnic minorities are underrepresented. Just 6 per cent of MPs are from a visible ethnic minority background, compared with 13 per cent of the population according to the 2011 census. Although the first ethnic minority MP was elected in 1841, there were none in the fifty years from 1929 to 1979.

Things have improved a lot since then, but initially only slowly. Hard-fought internal battles preceded the election of Labour's first ethnic minority MPs in 1987. It was not until 2001 that the number of ethnic minority Labour MPs reached double figures. The Conservatives never had more than two visible minority MPs at a time until eleven were elected in 2010. The total number of ethnic minority MPs took a further leap from twenty-seven in 2010 to forty-one in 2015 (seventeen Conservative, twenty-three Labour and one SNP).

There was a corresponding slow but then accelerating rise in the number of ethnic minority candidates since the 1970s. By 2001 the number for the Conservatives, Labour and Liberals combined was sixty-six, then 113 in 2005, 138 in 2010 and 162 in 2015. Across all parties there were at least 230 ethnic minority candidates in 2015.

More ethnic minorities are willing to stand, parties are more willing to nominate them and, crucially for representation, place them
in winnable and even safe seats. Is this because voters are increasingly accepting of non-white politicians?

Surveys have shown a decline in the numbers of people admitting
to racial prejudice – so if they are telling the truth we should expect
people to vote in a less racist way than in the past. One way to test
this is to examine whether parties suffer a relative drop in support
when they field an ethnic minority candidate. Studies of this kind
in the 1980s found mixed results, in part because the low number of
ethnic minority candidates standing made it hard to separate out a
common pattern from individual seat idiosyncrasies. However, from
1992 and pretty consistently through to 2015, constituency results suggest that when either of the two main parties switches from a white
to an ethnic minority candidate in seats where there are relatively few
ethnic minority residents then they suffer an average electoral penalty of two to three percentage points. There is no such discrepancy
in the seats with the most ethnic minority voters.

This pattern suggests (some) white voters continue to prefer voting for
white candidates, and also that (some) ethnic minorities may discrimi-
nate in favour of other minorities. Constituency results, however, are not
enough to confirm this because they cannot show how individual votes
depend on the ethnicity of candidates after accounting for other factors
affecting vote choices. Also, constituency analysis is vulnerable to what
is known as the 'ecological fallacy', where we try to infer the behaviour
of individuals based on differences in average behaviour across areas
with different social characteristics. We might well assume that if
areas with large ethnic minority populations behave more favourably
towards ethnic minority candidates, this is the result of ethnic minority voters being more likely to vote for those candidates, but we don't
know this. It may instead be that white voters in such areas are less racist.

One way of getting around this is to survey individual voters. Not to ask them whether they are happy to vote for minority candidates, but to see whether their vote choices are correlated with candidate ethnicity after controlling for other factors that affect vote choice. To be able to identify small but politically important differences in probabilities we need a random sample of several thousand voters covering most if not all constituencies with minority candidates. For ethnic minority voters, such a survey is only available for the 2010 general election.

When you analyse this data you find that ethnic minority candidates suffered an average electoral penalty of about four points at the hands of white voters.

But not all ethnic minority candidates are equally discriminated against – and not all white voters engage in racial discrimination at the ballot box. Muslim candidates were particularly likely to be discriminated against, by the three-quarters of white voters who expressed negative feelings about immigration. This Islamophobia at the ballot box accounts for just over half of the overall ethnic electoral penalty. Whereas non-Muslim minority candidates appear to suffer an average penalty of two points, that for Muslims is as much as eight percentage points.

And while on average white voters favour white candidates, in general, ethnic minority voters do not favour ethnic minority candidates. The exception is a clear co-ethnic effect for voters from a Pakistani background, who favoured candidates from the same background. This is not a process of Muslim voters for Muslim candidates, but something specific to the Pakistani community (and perhaps the Bangladeshi community too, although there were too few Bangladeshi candidates to be sure) and often linked to kinship networks.

Such community mobilisation is controversial among second and third generation Pakistanis and may now be in decline, and there was no sign of Indian heritage voters disproportionately supporting Indian heritage candidates, or black voters favouring black candidates (either generally or considering black African and black Caribbean heritage groups separately).

Given that most ethnic minorities want there to be more ethnic minority MPs and their shared experience of discrimination, the relative lack of co-minority voting is perhaps surprising. The main explanation lies in the strength of the Labour Party among minorities. Since Labour are seen as the best party to defend minority interests, minorities tend not to abandon white Labour candidates to vote for a non-white candidate from another party, even if that candidate is from the voter's own ethnic group.

As a result of all this, constituencies with relatively large ethnic minority populations tend to vote Labour and ethnic minority candidates do relatively well in them. Taking advantage of this situation, Labour have increased minority representation by placing ethnic minority candidates in ethnic minority seats with little or no cost in votes. By contrast, in seeking to modernise and diversify his party, David Cameron's only choice was to place ethnic minority candidates in overwhelmingly white areas and suffer the electoral penalty because (some) white voters, and not just Conservatives, still prefer their MPs to be white.

It is a puzzle as to why studies have not shown a decline in the ethnic electoral penalty since the 1980s, given the decline in racism in general. There is an old quip that gender equality means female MPs should be just as bad as the male ones. Perhaps the average quality of ethnic minority candidates has gone down as parties have been more willing to accept them, and so the ethnic penalty is not balanced out by the better quality of ethnic minority candidates in the way it used to be. We shall never know, and there are other possible explanations. But it is clear that racial discrimination remains a problem at the ballot box as in other walks of life.

FURTHER READING

For a discussion of the decline in racism internationally (among many other inter-esting things) see Steven Pinker's *The Better Angels of Our Nature* (Penguin, 2012). The analyses of constituency results referred to above come from the appendices by John Curtice and others in the so-called Nuffield election study series, of which the latest is Philip Cowley and Dennis Kavanagh's *The British General Election of 2015* (Palgrave Macmillan, 2016). The survey data analysis referred to is from 'Candidate Ethnicity and Vote Choice in Britain' (*British Journal of Political Science*, 2015) by Stephen D. Fisher et al.

—CHAPTER 8—

Apathy or alienation? The mystery of the missing young voters

Stuart Fox

Why have young people stopped voting in droves? They have long been less engaged with politics than their elders, but things have become much worse recently. The most recent generation – the so-called 'Millennials' who were born after 1982 and who came of age politically at the turn of the millennium – has set new standards, with electoral turnout well below that of their parents and grandparents at the same age. The British Election Study shows, for example, that around 57 per cent of Millennials reported voting in the 2015 general election, compared with an average of 79 per cent of older generations. When many Millennials were first voting in 2005, around 49 per cent cast a ballot, compared with an average of 74 per cent of older generations. The equivalent figures for the '90s generation in 1997 were 64 per cent and 82 per cent; for the '80s generation in 1987 were 71 per cent and 82 per cent; and for the '60s/'70s generation in 1974 were 80 per cent and 89 per cent.

The conventional explanation is that Millennials care about the issues of the day, but feel excluded from traditional party politics. They are not, therefore, apathetic about politics, but rather are alienated from it. This wisdom is repeatedly invoked by those promoting policy efforts to increase youth turnout, and challenging it has become controversial. Suggesting that the Millennials' low turnout might stem from a lack of interest rather than alienation has become associated with blaming the young for the failures of the political elite – and thus letting politicians off the hook.

The conventional wisdom, however, is wrong. For one thing, it relies on an impoverished understanding of 'political alienation' – a phrase that many people use, but few bother to define. The American political scientist Ada Finifter distinguished three types of political alienation in a work in 1970: i) powerlessness (feeling unable to influence the political process); ii) normlessness (feeling that the rules governing fair political interaction are not being respected); and iii) meaninglessness (a lack of confidence that one can find meaning in politics because of a lack of understanding). Political apathy, by contrast, refers to a lack of interest in politics. An alienated individual desires to participate, but that desire is undermined by their estrangement from the process; an apathetic individual has little desire to begin with.

There are further thorny problems with testing the conventional wisdom even once we have our definitions straight, as a voter's apathy or alienation at a given moment can reflect several factors we need to account for. It could be a result of their stage in the life cycle (given that political interest is lower among 'youth'). It could also reflect historic circumstances or events, such as a war or a scandal. Or it could reflect distinctive experiences or influences during the early years of adulthood when values are often formed – something which is often said to explain the Millennials' 'alienation'.

Using the British Social Attitudes survey, we can get an idea of how these three processes might be affecting the Millennials' apathy and alienation. Using statistical models, we can estimate the chances of a Millennial being 'highly apathetic' (that is, having little or no interest in politics) or 'highly alienated' (agreeing that they have no influence over politics, that the political process does not operate justly, or that they cannot understand politics) once we have accounted for the life cycle and historic context. The table shows the likelihood of each generation being highly apathetic or alienated once these factors have been accounted for.

The Millennials do stand out – but their distinctiveness is the opposite of the conventional wisdom. When compared with their elders, they aren't engaged but alienated, they are satisfied but apathetic. Millennials have a 43 per cent likelihood of being 'highly apathetic' compared with an average of 35 per cent among older generations. This makes them the most apathetic generation in the electorate, even after accounting for their youth. Their apathy also reflects a generational trend of falling interest in politics; the '90s generation, for example, are the second most apathetic generation in the electorate, the '80s generation the third most.

AVERAGE LIKELIHOOD OF HIGH APATHY/ ALIENATION OF POLITICAL GENERATIONS

	APATHY	POWERLESSNESS	NORMLESSNESS	MEANINGLESSNESS
Pre-War (pre-1926)	34%	67%	75%	65%
Post-War (1926–1945)	33%	71%	79%	67%
'60s–'70s (1946–1957)	32%	66%	75%	60%
'80s (1958–1968)	36%	62%	77%	62%
'90s (1969–1981)	39%	59%	75%	63%
Millennials (post-1982)	43%	56%	70%	69%

Source: British Social Attitudes, 1986–2012. Years in brackets indicate the period during which generation was born.

The Millennials are also the *least* alienated on two of the three measures. Their 56 per cent likelihood of expressing low confidence in the responsiveness of the political process is the lowest of any generation,

and compares with an average of 65 per cent among older generations. Similarly, their 70 per cent likelihood of expressing little faith
in the integrity of the political process – while still high – is also the
lowest, below the 76 per cent average of older cohorts. The one way
in which the Millennials are distinctly alienated is meaninglessness.
They have a 69 per cent likelihood of expressing the lowest level of
confidence in their knowledge of politics, compared with an average
of 63 per cent among older cohorts.

The conventional wisdom is that Britain's Millennials are fired up
about political issues but lack confidence in the political process. In fact,
the opposite is true: Millennials express greater confidence in the
operation of the political process than their elders (though not their
understanding of it), while being the most politically apathetic generation in the history of British survey research. As alienation is thus
not the reason for low youth turnout, policy responses designed to
combat alienation are unlikely to succeed. Instead, the focus should
shift onto understanding why Millennials find politics so boring.

FURTHER READING

Examples of research arguing that the Millennials are a politically alienated generation include 'Uninterested Youth? Young People's Attitudes towards Party Politics in
Britain' by Matt Henn and colleagues (*Political Studies*, 2005), and *Young People and
Politics in the UK: Apathy or Alienation?* by David Marsh and colleagues (Palgrave
Macmillan, 2007). More information on the definition and dimensions of political
alienation can be found in Ada Finifter's 'Dimensions of Political Alienation' (*Amer-
ican Political Science Review*, 1970), and Patricia Southwell's 'Political Alienation:
Behavioural Implications of Efficacy and Trust in the 2008 US Presidential Election'
(*Review of European Studies*, 2012).

CHAPTER 9

Like bears do: turnout and the weather

Galina Borisyuk

Conventional wisdom has it that the weather on polling day affects voter turnout. Surely, the reasoning goes, if the rain is bucketing down (this is Britain, after all) this must deter some voters. And if it does, which party will suffer?

The problem with this assumption is that there is no evidence for it. Not a shred. Besides, if it is raining in one part of the country it may be cloudy in another and a small minority may even be enjoying some brief sunshine as they visit the polling station.

But if we could examine the relationship between nature and turnout how would we do it? The answer – as with so many things in life – is to be found in local council by-elections. These are caused by the resignations or deaths of sitting councillors. Unlike their parliamentary equivalents there are hundreds of these contests each year. And crucially, they take place across the year.

Obviously, weather records for each by-election are unavailable but the level of daylight hours is a known quantity and conveniently is the same for all years and does not vary much across such a small island.

One study reported findings based on observing turnout at 5,193 by-elections between January 1983 and December 1999. It became clear that nature *did* matter. Turnout took a noticeable dip from late October onwards with the onset of winter, only to recover again in the spring. Turnout averaged 37 per cent during April–June but only 31 per cent in the three darkest months from November to January.

At the beginning of this century, however, politicians began to interfere in the natural rhythm of voter turnout. Electors generally were becoming more reluctant to participate and so, the politicians reasoned, voting should become easier. Various experiments were begun – voting in supermarkets, voting by phone or online and even on Sundays. Only one trial produced promising results – postal voting.

Postal voter registration was therefore made easier and became more widespread. At the 1997 general election 2.3 per cent of the electorate could vote by post. By 2015 the figure had risen to 16.4 per cent. Moreover, postal voters were more likely to vote than people who vote in person. Turnout averaged 63 per cent among electors voting at polling stations in 2015 but 82 per cent for people voting by post.

The policy of extending the right to a postal vote produces something that is highly prized by social scientists – a natural experiment. How would by-election voters now behave when not required to venture outdoors (except to post their vote)? Would seasonal factors associated with the earth's passage around the sun cease to have an impact upon voter turnout?

Since 2000 approximately four thousand council by-elections have taken place. In these the difference in average turnout between the November–January and April–June months has reduced to four percentage points compared to a six-point difference previously. It is difficult to draw a firm conclusion from that broad statistic and so we need to consider the results in slightly more detail.

The figure shows seasonal components of monthly variations in turnout using December as the base month. The horizontal axis is divided into twelve monthly segments while the vertical axis measures the increase in monthly average turnout from the December baseline. The black and grey lines represent the periods before and after the introduction of postal voting.

There are similarities and differences in these lines.

They each show turnout reaching its peak in May with the lowest turnout in December and so some seasonality remains. But, while the black line shows turnout steadily increasing from January onwards and staying relatively high into June, the grey line by contrast reveals more of a spike in May. These differences are statistically significant. While the movement in the black line is smoother, apparently tracking the rise and fall of daylight hours, the grey line appears less natural, affected mainly by political campaigning for the May local elections.

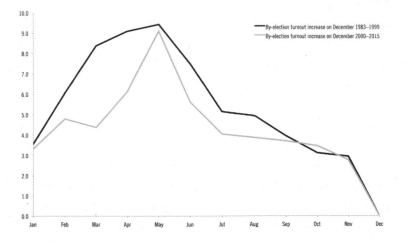

TURNOUT IN COUNCIL BY-ELECTIONS BEFORE AND AFTER POSTAL VOTING WIDENED

By-election turnout increase on December 1983–1999
By-election turnout increase on December 2000–2015

Voter participation, it appears, is no longer influenced by the warming rays of the sun but controlled more by the artificial glare of publicity as politicians and the media crank up interest in voting during the lead up to the May elections. This interest among electors is barely sustained beyond the short 'window of voting' as turnout takes a rapid tumble before stabilising between July and November.

Discovering that our hypothesis is largely correct and that changes in the natural seasons are no longer producing strong fluctuations in turnout should make us happy, but it doesn't, for two reasons. First, there is something rather nice, although maybe not altogether surprising, in discovering that people's electoral participation is shaped by nature. To see that relationship weaken is quite sad. The second reason for disappointment is because the data also reveals that electors, far from participating more, are actually participating less than before. The average by-election turnout was 33.5 per cent during 1983–99 but only 28.7 per cent from 2000. Without postal voting, of course, this decline in turnout would have been greater still, but even with postal voting it is still declining.

And the seasonal cycle, though reduced, has not disappeared altogether. Some voters still behave like bears. During the late spring and early summer they engage with the electoral process before hibernating for the winter. But it seems that many of these voters are becoming affected by political climate change, now spending far longer in hibernation than before and only briefly emerging for a quick dash to the polling station.

FURTHER READING

The original study of turnout was Colin Rallings et al.'s 'Seasonal Factors, Voter Fatigue and the Costs of Voting' (*Electoral Studies*, 2003). Postal voting is discussed in the Electoral Commission's *Delivering Democracy: The Future of Postal Voting* (2004). For empirical studies of the impact of weather in other countries see, for example, Mikael Persson et al.'s 'Does Election Day Weather Affect Voter Turnout? Evidence from Swedish elections' (*Electoral Studies*, 2014), Rob Eisinga et al.'s 'Weather Conditions and Voter Turnout in Dutch National Parliament Elections, 1971–2010' (*International Journal of Biometeorology*, 2012), and 'The Republicans Should Pray for Rain: Weather, Turnout and Voting in US Presidential Elections' (*Journal of Politics*, 2007) by Brad Gomez et al.

CHAPTER 10

The ghosts of Gower: death and voting

Kingsley Purdam

Ronnie Carroll, who died in April 2015 aged eighty, had two claims to fame. He was the only singer to have represented the UK in the Eurovision Song Contest two years in succession, with 'Ring-a-Ding Girl' in 1962 and 'Say Wonderful Things' the year after, coming fourth on both occasions. He also won votes at a British general election despite being dead.

At the time of his death, Carroll was standing for election in the marginal constituency of Hampstead and Kilburn. If a candidate from a registered party dies the election has to be stopped and re-run, but if an independent candidate like Carroll dies the election goes ahead. Despite his ambition to be a candidate who secured no votes, and despite the significant drawback of being dead, he secured 113 votes, more than one of his living competitors managed. It is perhaps little consolation that a candidate who dies during an election has their deposit returned.

Elsewhere, several dead candidates have been even more successful than Mr Carroll. In 2000, Democrat Mel Carnahan won a US Senate seat for Missouri several weeks after dying in an air crash.

In 2010, Jenny Oropeza won election to the California state senate several weeks after dying from cancer. And in the 2015 Myanmar election, the 54-year-old U Soe Myint, a candidate for Aung San Suu Kyi's National League for Democracy Party, won, despite dying from a heart attack during the campaign.

The dead also vote. Votes from the dead can end up in the ballot box for a number of reasons: administrative error, mistaken identity, the death of people shortly after sending their postal ballots off, or as a result of deliberate fraud. In 2012 in Nassau County in New York, 270 votes from dead people were identified, including one man who had voted fourteen times since his death. In the 2013 Zimbabwe general election, it was claimed that the electoral registers featured the names of two million dead people, including one record-breaking Methuselah aged 135. In the same year in Venezuela, there were reportedly more registered votes than there were people living in the country and 300,000 votes were cast in the names of dead people.

Most instances of the impact of death on elections are less dramatic, and the problem is more usually the sheer administrative complexity of mass electoral registers and the challenge of keeping them up to date, which means that many dead people remain on registers for some time after their demise. In the UK, the electoral registers are estimated to be around 90 per cent accurate, meaning millions of voters are not correctly registered at their current address – including some who have died since the register was last updated.

Of the around 50 million population aged eighteen and over in the UK, approximately 550,000 people (roughly 1 per cent of the population) die each year. That's around 1,500 people per day – although there are of course seasonal variations in mortality rates, as well as spatial ones (life expectancy in Conservative-held seats is higher than in Labour-held ones, for example). The main electoral registration process usually closes around two weeks before polling day (seventeen days in 2015), though it closes nearer to polling day for those who want to request postal or proxy votes. Even if we assume the electoral register is fully accurate when it closes (which we know is not the case) around 25,500 potential voters could die between the date when the main registration closes and polling day. If we only focus on the already registered electorate of 46.4 million people, this figure falls to around 21,500 potential voters.

Previously, this would not have been much of an issue. Sure, the dead might remain on the electoral roll, and this might make them prime targets for those who wish to vote fraudulently, given that there is no risk of the real voter turning up and causing a scene. But this wasn't exactly a major concern.

The increasing use of postal voting, however, adds to the likelihood of dead people voting, because they may have already cast their vote before dying. In 2015, 7.6 million people requested postal votes, and (as noted in Chapter 9) these are much more likely to be cast than in-person votes. With the main postal voting registration closing sixteen days before polling day and with the need to send a postal vote at least the day before polling day in order to ensure it arrives in time to be included, there is a possibility that around 3,000 potential postal voters could die before (if they have completed the ballot paper but not posted it) or after posting their vote but ahead of polling day. This is only an approximate figure. People who are about to die might be ill and less likely to vote, even by post. But on the other hand, postal voting request rates are disproportionately high among older people, and so the total number of deaths may well be higher.

Could dead voters have determined the outcome in any constituency race in the last election in the UK? Probably not – at least, not yet. The number of dead voters per constituency will be low. A figure of 3,000 across the country represents around five people per constituency. Even if we assume all of these people voted in one direction (unlikely) they will not have been numerous enough to determine the outcome in any constituency in 2015. We can safely say that Bryon Davies, the present Conservative MP for Gower in Wales, who has the smallest majority – just twenty-seven votes – did not emerge victorious solely due to the votes of the dead (even though areas of south Wales have some of the lowest life expectancies and lowest healthy life expectancies in the UK). Similarly, the 2016 EU referendum was won by a wide enough margin – of over 1 million – that dead voters could not have swung it one way or the other.

However, with an ageing population (the population over eighty years and older is projected to increase to eight million by 2050), higher turnout among older people, long-term inequalities in life expectancy across different areas and a growing use of postal votes, the chances are that some future constituencies' results will turn on the choices made by the recently departed.

FURTHER READING

Information on electoral registration regulations in the UK is available in 'Elections and Individual Electoral Registration' (Association of Electoral Administrators, 2015). For evidence of the quality of electoral registration and dead people being able to vote see *Election Initiatives* (Pew Trust, 2012). And for information on the use of psychics to see how historical figures would have voted see Chippendale and Horrie's *Stick It up Your Punter! The Uncut Story of the Sun Newspaper* (Heinemann, 1990).

'I always cheer up immensely if one is particularly wounding because I think, well, if they attack one personally, it means they have not a single political argument left.'

MARGARET THATCHER

—CHAPTER 11—

On the attack:
the role of
negative campaigning

Caitlin Milazzo

You would be hard pressed to find a legitimate political party or candidate who would admit to running a negative campaign. During the 2015 general election, leaders from all of Britain's major parties vehemently denied allegations of negativity, promising that their campaigns were – and would remain – positive. But what does it mean to 'go negative' in a campaign? The term is often used to refer to campaign messages that people deem derogatory, overly personal, or perhaps even untrue. In this way 'negative' is often equated to 'nasty'.

But political scientists generally take the view that campaign negativity is more about criticism and comparison than defamation. This includes a lot of perfectly valid criticism: on policy positions, qualifications or previous record. The content of such campaigning is almost always negative in the sense that it focuses on weaknesses of the opponent – people don't put out leaflets singing their opponents' praises – but it need not be ugly.

Even without being nasty, going negative has long been condemned as an electoral strategy. For one thing, voters say they hate it. In the United States, the idea that voters find negative campaigning distasteful has become so widely accepted that few pollsters even ask about it anymore. But voters don't just hate negative campaigning; they also think less of those who engage in it. Studies have shown that negative campaigning tends to backfire, lowering voters' evaluations of the author of the attack as well as its target. Negativity can also drive voters away from the political process: they lose interest in elections, and no longer want to take part in them. A series of influential studies by Stephen Ansolabehere and Shanto Iyengar found that individuals who were exposed to a negative advertisement were less likely to say they would vote in an election than those who had seen a positive ad. Moreover, those without strong partisan ties – that is, the critical 'swing' voters that can alter the outcome of an election – were most susceptible to these demobilising effects.

Given all this, it comes as no surprise that the leaders of Britain's political parties were continually promising positivity. Voters didn't believe them, though. Following the 2015 general election, two-thirds of the British public said that political parties and politicians were more concerned with fighting each other than with furthering the public's interest. And if we look at what parties actually said during the campaign, we see that the public were probably right. An analysis of more than 3,400 general election leaflets – the most common form of interaction that most British voters have with parties during the campaign – shows that, despite the leaders' promises, negativity was indeed widespread in 2015. Two-thirds of all of the leaflets examined contained a message about an opposing party or parties. As the figure below shows, in the case of Labour and the Liberal Democrats, the figure rises to over 80 per cent. Only the Greens and UKIP had less than half of their leaflets including at least one message about another party.

PHILIP COWLEY AND ROBERT FORD

PERCENTAGE OF LEAFLETS CONTAINING A MESSAGE
ABOUT AN OPPONENT, 2015

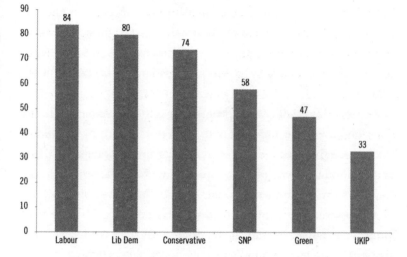

That UKIP's leaflets were the least negative may come as a surprise to many. Throughout the campaign, polls consistently showed
that more people believed UKIP was running a negative campaign than any other party. But asking voters to judge campaign
negativity is problematic, because our judgements about politics
tend to be influenced by our party identification – what is called
'partisan bias'.

In the context of negative campaigning, partisan bias means that
people who do not like a party are more likely to think that the party's campaign is negative, regardless of what the party actually says.
For example, a YouGov poll conducted during the final weeks of
the 2015 campaign showed that 51 per cent of survey respondents
thought UKIP was running a negative campaign. But only 4 per cent
of UKIP supporters thought this was the case. And UKIP wasn't the
only party suffering the effect of partisan bias; the campaigns of all

the major parties were rated more positively by their own supporters. When voters were asked about the tone of each campaign after the election, on average, UKIP supporters had a more positive impression of their party's campaign than the supporters of every other party except the SNP. However, few others shared these sentiments – the difference between the views of UKIP supporters and those that did not support the party was greater than the difference for any other party.

So negativity is widespread, but is this bad? Or does negative campaigning have some, well, positives? One recent study by Mattes and Redlawsk showed that while voters may say they hate negativity, they actually find negative information more useful – they see messages that tell them about an opponent's political record or highlight the issue differences between competitors, which can often provide more valuable resources to inform their decisions than the information that a party provides about its own platform. Voters may trust a candidate to provide a full account of her own strengths, but they don't believe she will be honest about her weaknesses. This is why voters find criticism useful – it gives them the full story and they are better able to make informed choices because of it.

Parties seem to recognise the greater value of negative information to voters, as they deploy more of it where contests are close: leaflets in British marginal constituencies were more likely to contain a negative message. In seats that were decided by less than 5 per cent of the vote, 75 per cent of the leaflets collected contained a negative message. In seats where a candidate won by more than forty points, less than 60 per cent of the leaflets had a negative message. Voters in the key marginals may see a nastier race, but perhaps as a consequence they are also able to make a more informed choice.

FURTHER READING

The majority of studies on negative campaigning focus on the United States. For an overview of this literature, see Richard Lau and Ivy Rovner's 'Negative Campaigning' (*Annual Review of Political Science*, 2009). Stephen Ansolabehere and Shanto Iyengar's *Going Negative: How Political Advertising Shrinks and Polarizes the Electorate* (Free Press, 1995) set the agenda and is still valuable. The edited volume by Nai and Walter *New Perspectives on Negative Campaigning: Why Attack Politics Matters* (ECPR Press, 2015) provides an introduction to the growing literature on negative campaigning outside the United States. *The Positive Case for Negative Campaigning* (University of Chicago Press, 2014), by Kyle Mattes and David P. Redlawsk, does what it says on the tin.

CHAPTER 12

Positive abstention: supporting none of the above

Chris Game

What happens when electoral supply doesn't match the voters' demands? The British Election Survey asked voters to rank from 0 to 10 the likelihood of their ever voting for each of the seven main political parties. The proportion of British citizens awarding at least one party a score of 8+ was lower than in twenty-one of the twenty-eight EU countries – and lower than anywhere in mainland western Europe.

Many potential voters evidently find none of the parties electorally attractive, and in that sense feel poorly represented by the existing options. It is a disorder – but of the system, not the voter. Our elections offer voters no positive way to express through the ballot box their dissatisfaction with all parties and candidates on offer.

Voters can stay at home, of course, as over a third of even those on the electoral register did in the past four general elections. Or we can avoid the hassle of registering altogether. Both inactions, though, have the usually unintended effect of endorsing the existing system and incumbents.

Inside the polling booth, our only recourse is deliberately to spoil the ballot paper, by voting for or against all candidates, writing vulgarities, or demonstrating our terrific sense of humour and artistry by drawing (invariably male) genitalia. But all these token gestures are similarly recorded as rejected ballots – on the ironic grounds of the voter's intention being 'uncertain', when frequently it could hardly be clearer.

In fairness, the humour of other countries' disenchanted voters is hardly Wildean in its sophistication. Scandinavians tend to regress to childhood. Finns 'spoil' their ballots by writing in names of favourite fictional characters – particularly Donald Duck, but also Captain Haddock from Hergé's Tintin, and Moominmamma from Tove Jansson's popular Moomin family books.

Disgruntled Swedes also have a DD fixation. Voters in all Sweden's party list elections can choose between three ballot papers, offering choice of party, of party and a named candidate, or a completely blank paper on which the voter writes in a party name. There are predictable regulars – the Beer Party, Jesus, Hitler and, more recently, the Zlatan Party, after Sweden's football captain, Zlatan Ibrahimović – but the undisputed long-term favourite is Kalle Anka, the Donald Duck Party.

Labelling it undergraduate humour would be insulting to students – and in more than the obvious sense. For most student union elections have a key feature to encourage reluctant voters that our national and local elections lack. If you don't think any candidate is worth your vote, then you can vote for RON, short for 'Re-Open Nominations'. And if, as can happen, RON wins or gets elected in a multi-member constituency, then the position is temporarily filled or remains vacant while nominations are indeed re-opened and the elections re-run.

As a means of positive abstention or expressly withholding consent,

RON is often aligned with the NOTA (None Of The Above) options that several countries attempt to operate. Even the acronyms, though, indicate their distinction. NOTA is about what happens in the ballot box and may, and often does, stop there; a few extra voters have participated, no harm done. RON is NOTA with consequences, necessarily about what happens next.

France has had a NOTA option since 1852, *le vote blanc* – the white or blank vote – which, following a daring 2014 reform, is now counted separately from, but still added to, other *nul* (invalid) votes. India's electronic NOTA option is similarly neutered. This exclusion from the counted total can matter; in France, for example, election to several offices, including the presidency, requires an absolute majority of votes cast. So the bigger a counted NOTA vote, the higher would be the majority required from the voters who support a candidate. It matters in Spain too, where they include *votos en blanco*, thereby raising the 3 per cent or 5 per cent bar of votes required for small parties to achieve representation.

NOTA's profoundest impact, though, was arguably east of the infamous Iron Curtain, where Lech Wałęsa – Polish trade union leader and later President and Nobel Peace Prize winner – has claimed it 'changed history'. By allowing voters to cross out Communist incumbents' names in at least semi-free elections in Poland (1989) and to the Soviet Congress of People's Deputies (1991), it 'proved how far people despised Communist rule and accelerated the entire decline of the Communists in Eastern Europe'.

In the UK in 2014 the Commons Political and Constitutional Reform Committee (PCRC) wasn't trying to hasten the end of Coalition rule, but, albeit radically, to increase voter turnout. The committee collated over 16,000 responses to several consultative voting reform surveys, with results that its members saw as certainly substantively, even if not statistically, significant.

RESPONSES TO THE PCRC CONSULTATION ON VOTER TURNOUT

RESPONSES IN ORDER OF YES % (DON'T KNOWS OMITTED)	YES %	NO %
'None of the Above' an option on ballot paper	72	21
Registering to vote a legal obligation	65	27
Able to vote online	58	32
Elections held at the weekend	50	23
Voting a legal obligation	46	46
Registration to vote up to and on Election Day	43	42
16- and 17-year-olds able to vote	40	51

With 72 per cent support, inclusion of a NOTA option was comfortably the most popular change to electoral arrangements considered by the committee, which recommended that the (next) government hold a public consultation solely on including a NOTA option on ballot papers for national elections and report to the House by May 2016.

That one of the next government's earliest acts was the PCRC's abolition says everything necessary about the immediate fate of its recommendation. There's also no knowing, beyond the media interest it would surely generate, what stimulus to turnout a NOTA option might actually produce. But currently the cause is in the noisy hands of, among others, NOTA UK and the campaigning organisation 38 Degrees, so it won't quietly disappear. NOTA, or even the student favourite, RON, could yet have their chance on British ballots one day.

FURTHER READING

Data on the Representation Gap is downloadable from 'Westminster Impact: BES Insights into 2015'. The most relevant reports of the Political and Constitutional Reform Committee are its fourth and sixth 2014–15 reports on *Voter Engagement in the UK*

(November 2014 and February 2015). *None of the Above* (Simon & Schuster, 2015) by Rick Edwards, host of BBC3's debate programme *Free Speech*, was one of the most interesting books published during the 2015 campaign. Bruno Kaufmann gives an insight into Sweden's 80+ per cent turnouts in a *Time* magazine article (5 November 2014). Last and obviously not least, check out NOTA UK's website, regular posts and archives.

CHAPTER 13

More politics, less voting: the internet paradox

Javier Sajuria

E ver since Barack Obama's election to the US presidency in 2008, commentators have claimed that traditional campaigning – and politics – have been changed for good. Online campaigns were said to be a central means to engage young people, helping to reverse the declines in youth turnout discussed in Chapter 8.

Some researchers have added to this hype by pointing to a link between the internet and political engagement, again particularly among youngsters. A widely reported mass experiment by Robert Bond and his colleagues used data from millions of Facebook users during Obama's first election to assess if informing people about whether their Facebook friends had voted could influence whether they themselves turned out. The authors found that it did – the more people who voted in a person's social network, the likelier they were to vote themselves. While it generated a lot of interest, this 'social media effect' was in fact very small: the increase in turnout was not higher than 0.3 per cent. Since then, other researchers have tried to assess the social media effect with similarly underwhelming results.

In 2014, the British Election Study posed a series of questions specifically designed to measure social connections, online or offline. This was the first time that such questions were asked of a national sample in the UK and the results – shown in the figure below – were surprising: people who mostly engage with their friends or acquaintances using the internet were *less* likely to vote than those who connect with others offline, or some combination of on and offline. This time, the effect was substantial: a reduction of up to 6 per cent in the probability of someone voting. However, those who combined their social connections online with face to face contact were around 3 per cent *more* likely to vote.

The internet seems to be more effective at fostering direct forms of participation, such as protesting, than traditional, mediated forms such as voting to elect representatives. One US study showed how the internet could be used to recruit people to participate in protests, particularly through friends or acquaintances. A Chilean study similarly showed that social media connections were especially efficient for getting young Chileans to protest against the government.

Why does social media encourage marching together for a cause, but not heading to the ballot box? In part, because people who used the internet for politics most intensively in the UK tend to hold very particular views about democracy. On the one hand, they think that democracy should be more horizontal and deliberative, that more power should be devolved to citizens and that representatives should be more accountable for their actions. That also means they prefer direct and deliberative forms of democracy to participating in representative exercises. On the other hand, the experience of instant communication and response online may undermine faith in the ability of the slower and murkier processes of traditional party politics to produce the outcomes they want, at the speed they desire. All of this encourages a street-based approach to politics, but discourages engagement with the traditional parties and the ballot box.

RELATIONSHIP BETWEEN SOCIAL CONNECTIONS
AND THE PROBABILITY OF VOTING
(A) ONLINE SOCIAL CONNECTIONS ONLY (TOP)
(B) COMBINED ONLINE AND OFFLINE SOCIAL CONNECTIONS (BOTTOM)

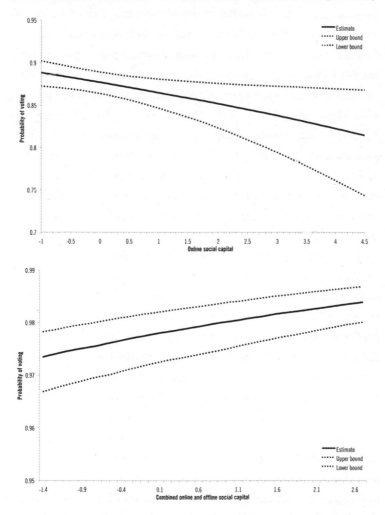

Note: Top figure shows how the increase in the number of social connections (online only) is related to a decrease in the probability of voting; bottom figure shows the effect of combined social connections (online and offline) on the probability of voting. The dotted lines represent the 95 per cent confidence intervals, which capture the statistical uncertainty about the estimated effect.

So the internet is helping people to engage in politics, just not in the way mainstream politicians might like. But this is not completely discouraging for traditional politics. While the negative effect on voting is observed among those who privilege online social connections, that is a relatively small group of voters, less than 10 per cent. Those who combine online and offline social connections represent a bigger share of the electorate, which means that political parties should look into diverse ways of engaging with their potential voters.

There have been several examples of successfully mixing offline and online engagement. The Obama campaigns in 2008 and 2012 combined in-person local meetings with an aggressive presence on social media, aiming to mobilise young people and ethnic minorities, both groups that were traditionally reluctant to engage in elections. A similar strategy was followed by Bernie Sanders in the 2016 Democratic primaries, aiming to engage young voters through a combination of online and offline campaigning.

In Europe, political initiatives such as PODEMOS in Spain or the Five Star Movement in Italy have shown how a balanced combination between traditional forms of political engagement and the use of new online tools can help build new political parties that attract high support from young voters. They have managed to breach the offline/online divide successfully by combining different platforms to engage and mobilise voters. The key is not to overestimate the role of new technologies for political action, but to learn how and when they can be useful, and how to combine them with traditional campaigning and organising techniques. Occasional internet users or those who are more likely to develop social connections online and offline at the same time may be more likely to engage productively with the political process than those who live their social lives mainly online. It may be of some comfort to politicians grappling with the new world of social media to learn that the persistent and hostile 'trolls' who haunt online forums are less important than the larger, and quieter, majority of social media users who also get out into the fresh air from time to time.

FURTHER READING

For an account of how new technologies are affecting collective action, see Bennett and Sergerberg's book *The Logic of Connective Action* (Cambridge University Press, 2013). For a detailed account on how organisations use new technologies to mobilise their audiences both online and offline, see *The MoveOn Effect* by David Karpf (Oxford University Press, 2012), and *Collective Action in Organizations* by Bimber et al. (Cambridge University Press, 2012). For an interesting description of how younger generations in Britain are using information and communication technologies for non-traditional political action, see 'Cuts, Tweets, Solidarity and Mobilisation: How the Internet Shaped the Student Occupations' by Yannis Theocharis (*Parliamentary Affairs*, 2012).

CHAPTER 14

Racing certainties: the value of political gambling

Matt Wall

I t has never been easier to take a punt on politics. Dozens of online and offline gambling companies offer markets on political outcomes, ranging from the deadly serious – such as the outcome of the EU referendum – to the faintly ridiculous, such as Boris Johnson's next sporting gaffe, where the favourite at the time of writing is 'crash while cycling', at odds of 1/3.

Gambling markets represent a sort of collective discussion on the likelihood of possible future events – with the capacity to quantify the opinions expressed through the odds that they make available. Odds can be straightforwardly translated into estimates of the probability that an event will occur – and move in response to shifts in betting patterns. Following the logic that 'it matters more when there's money on it', these odds are frequently said to be a better guide to the political future than opinion polls. But is this true?

On the whole, yes. Various studies have found that predictive markets based on political gambling activity generate forecasts that are at least as accurate as, and usually more accurate than, forecasts based on polling data alone. For instance, one study compared market predictions to 964 polls over five US presidential election cycles and found that market predictions were more accurate forecasts of the result 74 per cent of the time. The advantage of markets over polls becomes even more pronounced for long-term forecasts made more than 100 days in advance of the election.

Yet we should be cautious about placing too much faith in the opinions of political gamblers. Although betting markets are often correct in predicting electoral outcomes, they are by no means omniscient. Gamblers, like everyone else, get things wrong.

For example, while the betting markets did better than most pundits and pollsters in clearly predicting a Conservative victory over Labour in the 2015 elections (estimated at a likelihood of over 70 per cent by a suite of markets), they got it badly wrong when it came to predicting the Conservative majority, with most betting markets – just like the polls – rating a hung parliament at an average probability of over 90 per cent. They got it wrong the other way round in 2010 – being more confident than the polls that the Tories would secure a majority (wrongly, as we now know). They also got the 2016 EU referendum badly wrong, with final polls predicting a tight contest but the gambling markets putting the chances of a Leave vote at as low as 6 per cent when polls closed.

The most common reason why gambling markets fail is bad information. Since markets reflect the aggregation of opinions with money attached, and since opinions are based on available data, market predictions can be distorted by bad information. As discussed in Chapter 1, polling during the run-up to the 2015 general election systematically underestimated the Conservatives' vote share. The 2015 campaign also saw a large number of House of Commons projections based on polling data; these uniformly predicted a hung parliament. This was then reflected in the various 'overall majority' markets that sprang up on bookmaking and gambling market sites in the run-up to the election. More generally, one US study found evidence that, following the introduction of polling in the United States, betting markets became *worse* at predicting election outcomes, because flawed polls can crowd out other more useful forms of information that betting markets had captured in the pre-polling era.

A second reason why gambling markets may fail is that punters sometimes bet with their hearts rather than with their heads. A team of scholars led by Robert Forsythe found that traders in a 'political stock market' for the 1998 US presidential election exhibited significant judgement bias, tending to trade towards the candidate that they supported. This was the result of two mental processes that are well established in social psychology: the 'assimilation-contrast' effect, where one's preference for a given outcome affects the way in which new information about that outcome is processed, and the 'false-consensus' effect, where individuals tend to overestimate the extent to which their views are representative of the population.

The first type of bias was evident in trading following presidential debates, where partisan traders tended to be biased towards believing that 'their' candidate had performed well in the debate and traded accordingly. The second effect was also present, with supporters of a given candidate being considerably more likely to buy shares in that candidate than non-supporters.

Finally, people are just bad at estimating probabilities in systematic and predictable ways – even when there is money at stake. One of the most famous instances of this is known as the favourite–longshot bias. People tend to consistently (and persistently) overestimate the chances of longshot events coming to pass; all big lotteries rely on this bias. People seemingly can't imagine a possible but unlikely event without also overestimating how likely it is. We also tend to underestimate how likely probable events are. Favourites usually win – that's why they are favourites – but the human mind seems prone to imagining all the ways a likely winner might fail. Again, the error is mistaking the possible for the probable. Favourites can fall at the first fence, but most don't; if they did, bookies would not remain in business.

OBSERVED AND EXPECTED CHANCES OF WINNING IN 2010 CONSTITUENCY BETTING MARKETS

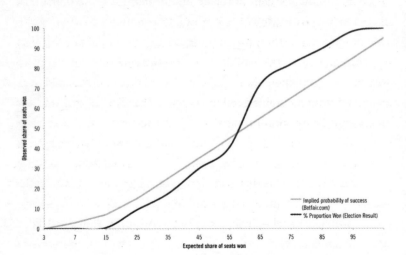

This bias has been demonstrated in numerous studies of gambling markets and had a marked effect on the constituency gambling markets in the 2010 election. The figure compares the chances punters gave various candidates of winning ahead of polling day, as captured via their odds on the betfair.com website (horizontal axis), with their actual rates of success (vertical axis). At the bottom left are the no-hopers; at the top right, the front-runners. The diagonal grey line maps out what we would expect to see if the punters were perfect forecasters – their estimates of candidates' chances would neatly match those candidates' rates of success. But that is not what we see in reality, as plotted by the black line. Instead what we get is an S-shaped curve. The bottom half of the 'S' are the longshots – punters are systematically too optimistic about them. For example, just 10 per cent of candidates rated by punters as having a one in four chance to win actually prevailed. When we get to front runners, the bias flips around, producing the upper curve of the 'S' – here candidates were a lot *more* successful than gamblers expected them to be. For example, 90 per cent of the candidates rated by the punters as having a three in four chance of winning won their races.

When Hunter S. Thompson was asked why he thought he knew so much about politics, he would reply that it was because he was smart – but he said he knew that was a lie. The real reason, he said, was 'because I'm an incurable gambling addict'. The act of putting money at stake on an opinion provides a strong incentive for researching and thinking about that opinion. But because political information is often incorrect, because people have preferences that affect how they process information and because we're often simply bad at estimating the probabilities of future events, the predictions of political betting markets should be taken with a substantial grain of salt.

FURTHER READING

For a discussion of the merits of polling versus gambling data see Robert S. Erikson and Christopher Wlezien's 'Are Political Markets Really Superior to Polls as Election Predictions?' (*Public Opinion Quarterly*, 2008) and 'Markets vs. Polls as Election Predictors: An Historical Assessment' (*Electoral Studies*, 2012), as well as David Rothschild's 'Forecasting Elections: Comparing Prediction Markets, Polls and their Biases' (*Public Opinion Quarterly*, 2009). For US presidential contests see Joyce Berg et al.'s 'Prediction Market Accuracy in the Long Run' (*International Journal of Forecasting*,

2008) and for constituency-level gambling, see Matthew Wall et al.'s 'What Are the Odds? Using Constituency-Level Betting Markets to Forecast Seat Shares in the 2010 UK General Elections' (*Journal of Elections, Public Opinion and Parties*, 2012). The Forsythe et al. paper is 'Anatomy of an Experimental Political Stock Market' (*American Economic Review*, 1992). Much of this discussion is based on work funded by the Arts and Humanities Research Council's Big Data Projects Call as part of its Digital Transformations theme.

CHAPTER 15

Why Labour needs a lot of earthquakes: Britain's vanishing marginal seats

Ron Johnston

A common criticism of the British electoral system is that general elections are won or lost in a relatively small number of constituencies. Most seats are 'safe', unlikely to change hands, and just a few thousand voters in the more marginal constituencies can make or break a party's chances.

That criticism is truer now than ever before. After the 1955 election there were 166 seats where a swing of less than five percentage points between Conservative and Labour could see them change hands. By 2001 there were 114; by 2010, only eighty-five; and after 2015, just seventy-four. There were fewer marginal constituencies after the 2015 contest than after any other post-war UK general election; at the next election Labour could win them all and still have fewer MPs than the Conservatives.

A corollary of fewer marginal seats is more safe ones where the incumbent party is virtually certain to win again. The graphs show this for the 2010 and 2015 elections. Constituencies are in six categories: very safe (either won or lost by more than twenty percentage points: the outer pairs of columns); fairly safe (won or lost by between ten and nineteen points); and marginal (won or lost by less than ten points: the central pairs of two columns).

MARGINS OF VICTORY/DEFEAT FOR CONSERVATIVES (TOP) AND LABOUR (BOTTOM) IN 2010 AND 2015

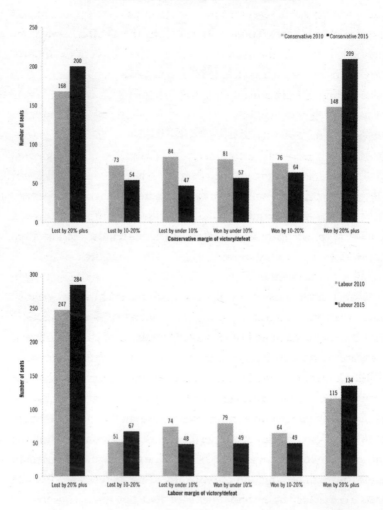

The top half of the figure shows the Conservatives' situation. In 2015 they had both more very safe seats, with majorities of 20 per cent or more over their nearest rival, and more hopeless causes, where they started twenty points or more behind the winning party, than in 2010 – around 200 seats in each category after the latter election. The story is similar for Labour (the bottom half), although in 2015 it had fewer very safe seats (around 130) than its main opponent and more hopeless causes (some 280), reflecting the fact that it was substantially behind in the overall vote share. The House of Commons' new third-largest party – the SNP – also now occupies many electoral strongholds. In 2015, it won half of its fifty-six seats by margins of twenty percentage points or more, and only six by less than ten.

A very large majority of British voters now lives in constituencies where only a political earthquake could dislodge the local incumbent. Of course, earthquakes can happen – the SNP's and the Liberal Democrats' performances in 2015 are testament to that – but they are rare. Without further such earthquakes in 2020, Labour will find it very hard to win a Commons majority then – whoever its leader is and whatever policies it espouses.

Great Britain's electoral geography has thus become much more polarised: more safe seats, fewer close contests. Each of the House of Commons' three largest parties – Conservative, Labour and SNP – now has a well-fortified homeland and a relatively small frontier of insecure seats where it might either advance or be dislodged.

The Conservative and Labour combined vote share hardly changed between the 2010 and 2015 general elections, when the main changes in the voting pattern were in support for the smaller parties. Nevertheless the geographies of support for those smaller parties in 2015 meant that outside Scotland, Labour and the Conservatives benefited most, through the creation of more safe seats. In Scotland, the safe seats were all held by the SNP; even for Labour, Scotland's hegemonic party for several decades before the SNP surge, the chances of winning any there in 2020 are very slight.

In England, many of the new safe seats resulted from the collapse in Liberal Democrat support virtually everywhere. In 2010 the Conservatives and Liberal Democrats occupied the first two places in forty marginal constituencies; nineteen of them became very safe, and a further thirteen fairly safe Conservative seats in 2015 as the Lib Dems endured the largest vote collapse for any party in modern British political history. The same was true in seats fought between Labour and the Liberal Democrats: thirteen of the twenty-seven Lab–Lib Dem marginals after the 2010 election became very safe for Labour in 2015, and a further eight fairly safe.

This collapse in the number of marginal seats involving the Liberal Democrats created more safe Conservative and Labour constituencies because it was not offset by a comparable surge in concentrated support for other parties. Although UKIP's vote share grew from 3.2 to 12.9 per cent between 2010 and 2015, and the Greens' from 0.9 to 3.8 per cent, these increases were fairly uniform across the country. A substantial Liberal Democrat advance from 1992 on was concentrated in a relatively small number of constituencies, many of which they won or made competitive. But with a few exceptions neither UKIP nor the Green Party won sufficient support either to win a seat or come a reasonably close second (UKIP came within 10 per cent of the winner in just three constituencies, and the Greens in just one). UKIP may have come second in 120 seats but it was so far behind that for any seats to change hands at the next election would need a swing away from the incumbent party of an intensity rarely experienced, and certainly not across a substantial number of constituencies.

Thus the Liberal Democrat collapse in many English constituencies created a wider gap between the incumbent party and the local runner up. And the SNP's advance had exactly the same impact – except that it occupied all of Scotland's fifty safe seats.

The effect of all of this is to reduce the chances of substantial change at the next election, even after the reduction from 650 to 600 constituencies after the forthcoming boundary redistribution. Spatial polarisation creates electoral stagnation – the consequence could be a further decade of Conservative hegemony. Unless there is a major Liberal Democrat revival, and/or an SNP collapse, and/or a substantial UKIP surge, and/or a very significant swing from the Conservatives to Labour, the situation at the next election will be more MPs than ever before presiding over local electoral fortresses, and storming the battlements to win a marginal seat will be a bigger challenge for their opponents than at previous elections.

FURTHER READING

On the declining number of marginal constituencies see the chapter 'A Return to Normality? How the Electoral System Operated' by John Curtice in *Britain Votes 2015* (Oxford University Press, 2015), and on the division of the country into different types of contest see Ron Johnston and Charles Pattie's 'The British General Election of 2010: A Three-Party Contest – or Three Two-Party Contests?' (*Geographical Journal*, 2011) and 'Britain's Changed Electoral Map in and beyond 2015: The Importance of Geography' (*Geographical Journal*, 2016), by Ron Johnston et al..

'Politics would be a helluva good business if it weren't for the goddamned people.'

RICHARD NIXON

CHAPTER 16

Guess who's coming to dinner?
Romance across party lines

Robert Ford

In August 2015, Labour leadership candidate Andy Burnham was spotted at an anti-austerity rally sporting a T-shirt with the slogan 'Never Kissed A Tory'. We do not know how many such opportunities Mr Burnham has spurned, or how he checked, but we can assume his choice of T-shirt indicates an endorsement of Tory avoidance as a romantic strategy. Mr Burnham not only disapproves of sleeping with the enemy, he wears this disapproval as a badge of pride.

He is far from alone in this judgement. A 2012 survey asked people how they would feel about their children marrying the supporters of different parties, detailed in the table below. Roughly a quarter of Labour voters said they would be upset if their child wished to marry a Conservative, even more than are upset by the prospect of a UKIP-voting in-law (23 per cent). Conservatives, by contrast, are more sanguine about political arguments over Christmas dinner. Around 12 per cent find the idea of their children marrying a Labour supporter upsetting.

The pattern repeats itself with newspaper readership. Left-leaning voters are more upset by the prospect of a *Daily Mail*- or

Sun-reading in-law than right-wing voters are about inter-marriage with *Guardian*istas or *Mirror* readers. Liberal Democrat voters in particular get very upset at the idea of family ties with people who read anything other than *The Guardian*.

Tolerance and inclusiveness are normally associated with the liberal left, whereas the right tends to regard difference with more suspicion. This is indeed what we see: Labourites and (particularly) Liberal Democrats are more accepting of a wide range of other social groups – ethnic and religious minorities, criminal and benefit claimants, among others – than Conservative voters. Why are left-liberal voters more socially tolerant yet more politically intolerant?

One possible explanation is simply that political intolerance is more acceptable to express, and so people are more willing to admit to it. This is undoubtedly true, for elite politicians at least: a T-shirt like Mr Burnham's could end a political career if targeted at an ethnic or religious group. However, it seems such concerns are not shared by all left or liberal voters, many of whom are also happy to express intolerance towards groups such as Muslims. And even if political intolerance is more acceptable to express in many social circles, this doesn't explain why left-wingers have more of it in the first place.

Another possibility is that supporters of parties out of power become more intolerant of those who backed the in-crowd. This could explain the 2012 Labour results, yet earlier surveys suggest Labour voters were even more politically intolerant in 2008, when Labour were in power.

Perhaps the source of political intolerance is less to do with the dynamics of power and popularity, and more to do with the information conveyed by the parties as group identities. All social groups exist in people's minds as a set of stereotypes. Parties are no different – surveys have revealed remarkably stable and powerful stereotypes about different parties' supporters. Greater intolerance of Conservative in-laws may reflect stronger negative stereotypes about Conservative voters. The power of stereotypes also explains why newspaper choice evokes similarly powerful but politically uneven reactions – the left stereotype of *Daily Mail* and *Sun* readers as bigoted, knuckle-dragging Neanderthals is more lurid than the right-wing image of *Guardian* readers as sanctimonious, pseudo-radical middle-class teachers.

SHARE OF PARTIES' 2010 VOTERS UPSET AT THE PROSPECT OF IN-LAWS WITH VARIOUS CHARACTERISTICS

SOCIAL GROUP	LABOUR	CONSERVATIVE	LIBERAL DEMOCRAT	OVERALL
PARTISANSHIP				
Labour voter	1	12	4	5
Liberal Democrat voter	10	5	6	7
Conservative voter	25	1	9	11
UKIP voter	23	10	32	18
Ethnic groups				
Black person	10	26	3	14
Indian	23	20	12	18
Immigrant	28	27	12	23
RELIGIOUS GROUPS				
Catholic	5	8	12	8
Atheist	11	10	5	9
Muslim	38	43	19	35
OTHER				
Someone living on state benefits	37	61	43	47
Someone with a criminal record	51	58	47	51

Source: YouGov, 2012

Political intolerance, then, reflects the fact that parties are not just things people vote for at election time. They are social groups, and voting for them is not a simple matter of choosing between potential leaders or menus of policies. It is a social act which, for many, affirms or reaffirms who they are (and, equally, who they are *not*). People form and reinforce with each other positive stereotypes about the parties they support, and negative stereotypes about the parties they oppose.

This can pose problems. If you think your party is composed of the just and the true, while the other side are crooks and liars, you're unlikely to judge either side fairly. So it proves. Voters tend to remember and highlight the successes of their own tribe, while forgetting or explaining away the triumphs of their opponents. What is more, voters who express enthusiasm for a policy in isolation turn against it if it is associated with their political enemies, seemingly reasoning that it can't be a good idea after all if the 'bad guys' favour it.

When such thinking becomes really intense, it can spill over from politics into other social fields. The partisan zealot searches for political motives everywhere. Such thinking risks corroding public trust by encouraging the belief that sectional motives are paramount in all parts of public life. Partisan zealots can also harm public institutions – politicians who believe all decisions are politically motivated can thereby justify using partisan loyalty rather than individual merit as the criterion for appointing the decision makers.

While it comes with risk, partisan passion is also a tempting campaign resource for politicians. Attacking the enemy can be a much easier way to stoke up supporters than presenting your own positive offer. Yet politicians who indulge this temptation reinforce stereotypes and deepen distrust, which in the long run can end up posing serious problems for them all. In America, mutual partisan hatred now threatens the basic operation of government. A stable democracy requires that supporters of each party show at least a minimum of trust and respect towards their opponents. British democracy might therefore be a little bit better if Mr Burnham had kissed a few Tories.

FURTHER READING

A comprehensive analysis of the power of partisan intolerance can be found in
Iyengar et al.'s 'Affect, not Ideology: A Social Identity Perspective on Polarisation'
(*Public Opinion Quarterly*, 2012). Will Dahlgreen published a recent discussion of the
greater political intolerance of left-wingers using YouGov data from Britain and the
US in 'Left-Wingers Like to Keep It in the Family' (2016). John Sides provides a nice
summary of the distorting power of partisan stereotypes in his 'Democrats are gay,
Republicans are rich: Our stereotypes of political parties are amazingly wrong' (2016).
If you fancy a longer read, the best book on partisanship as a form of social identity
is *Partisan Hearts and Minds* by Donald Green et al. (Yale University Press, 2002).

CHAPTER 17

Playing on home turf: the importance of issue ownership

James Dennison

Voters consistently rank some parties as better at handling certain issues than others. In the United States, for example, voters regularly name the Republicans as the best party to deal with security and crime, whereas the Democrats are generally ranked as the best party on social security and education. When voters habitually think of a party as being better equipped to deal with an issue, we say the party 'owns' the issue. If the issues that a party owns are those that a voter cares about, this should dramatically boost the voter's chance of voting for that party – voters should gravitate to the parties thought to be best at solving the problems that matter most to them.

The distribution of issue ownership tends to be fairly stable across time, both because voters' perceptions about parties are difficult to change and because of the considerable resources that parties invest into maintaining their reputations on issues where they are strong. Moreover, parties have an incentive to emphasise the importance of their owned issues in order to fully exploit their political value.

Historic and long-running examples of issue ownership in the UK include Labour on health and education and the Conservatives on the economy and crime, as evidenced by hundreds of polls over the last decades. But changes do happen. In the 1990s, following the European Exchange Rate Mechanism crisis, the Conservative Party's competence on economic matters began to be questioned just at the time that Labour was committing itself to a more moderate economic approach – and the result was a rare shift in issue ownership. More recently, the Conservatives, who have consistently owned immigration since the 1970s, have lost the issue to the populist right UK Independence Party (UKIP).

BEST PARTY TO HANDLE IMMIGRATION, 2010–2015

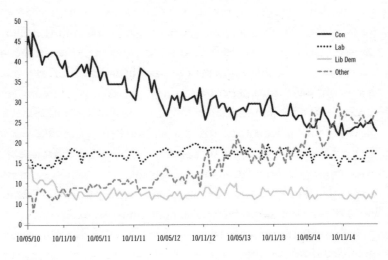

Source: YouGov Issues Tracker

In just five years, over the course of the 2010–2015 parliament, the Conservatives went from having a thirty-point lead as the best party to handle immigration to being behind UKIP and only ten points ahead of Labour. Why has this happened? Five years of a Conservative-led government presiding over high immigration levels despite pledging to bring them down has done lasting damage to the party's reputation on the issue: a majority of voters in 2015 blamed the government for high levels of immigration and believed that the party neither cared about the issue nor wanted to reduce immigration. Furthermore, a majority of voters believed that David Cameron's party would be unsuccessful at reducing immigration, even if it tried.

This loss of ownership is particularly harmful to the Conservatives because immigration is at the top of the political agenda. In December 2015, 63 per cent of voters believed that immigration was one of the top three issues affecting the UK, far ahead of the economy on 39 per cent. As in a number of other European countries, a populist right party seems to have gained ownership over one of the major prizes of contemporary politics. The translation of ownership into votes is fairly clear. Simply multiplying the proportion of the electorate who considered immigration to be the most important issue in May 2015 (52 per cent), by the proportion who believed UKIP would be best on that issue (27 per cent), gives an accurate prediction for UKIP's vote share in the general election: just under 14 per cent.

The capture of a major policy issue is a particularly impressive feat for UKIP, not just in terms of their swiftness in doing so and the issue's relative importance, but because UKIP is still not, and may never be, one of the major parties. By way of comparison, the Liberal Democrats – with a much longer history and much larger Westminster presence – were *never* ranked as the best party to deal with a major policy issue between 2005 and 2015, though they did come close on education and taxation prior to the 2010 general election.

How can we expect the change of ownership of immigration to affect future elections? So long as immigration remains an important issue, UKIP will have a strong foundation for support. It seems unlikely that the Conservatives will be able to win back public trust on immigration for some time because people often evaluate immigration policy via immigration levels, which were in large part outside of the control of the British government so long as the UK remained a member of the European Union – and will remain so in many of the possible post-EU scenarios.

In fact, the Conservatives will likely campaign far less on immigration in future than they have done in the past and, rather than waste resources on an issue owned by a competing party, instead shift their focus to the issues they still own, such as the economy and unemployment. Such a rational strategic move would only serve to reinforce UKIP's position as the 'best' party on the subject. Labour and the Liberal Democrats also lack the necessary credibility to offer any real competition to UKIP's ownership of the subject. Therefore, aside from UKIP, no major British party has an incentive to campaign on the subject. Despite immigration's extremely high salience with many voters, a new equilibrium may arise that replicates the campaign of 2015 in its relative quiet on the subject. Immigration will be less debated than ever, as the issue is essentially 'parked' with a non-governing party. Ironically, public discontent over immigration has been so strong that it has led to the emergence of a new party, yet, now that the damage has been done on the issue, the best thing the established parties can do is to let the issue's owners, UKIP, with their single Member of Parliament, do all the talking on the subject.

FURTHER READING

The concepts and previous empirical findings on 'issue ownership' are developed in 'Introduction: Issue Ownership' by Jonas Lefevere et al. (*West European Politics*, 2015) and Éric Bélanger and Bonnie Meguid's 'Issue Salience, Issue Ownership and Issue-Based Vote Choice' (*Electoral Studies*, 2008). For UKIP and immigration, see James Dennison and Matthew Goodwin's 'Immigration, Issue Ownership and the Rise of UKIP' (*Parliamentary Affairs*, 2015).

—CHAPTER 18—

More similar than you think: parallel publics and the issue agenda

Jane Green

I t is easy to imagine that the supporters of different parties have dramatically different political outlooks. Parties' most vocal supporters
often portray their policy priorities as fundamental matters of prin-
ciple. Indeed, one might think that party supporters are defined by
their backing for particular definitional policies. This is clearly true
for a vocal and passionate minority of members and activists, but is
it true of parties' broader support bases?

A closer look suggests a lot more overlap between different parties'
supporters than we might expect. Different political tribes exist, but they
often share similar priorities, and respond in the same way to events
and to the ebb and flow of politics. Researchers call this phenomenon
'parallel publics': while party supporters can be distinctive, they tend, on
the whole, to respond in a similar way to different events and political
stimuli. When public support for more government spending is rising, it tends to be rising for all groups of people whatever their political
persuasion. People who would see themselves as centre-left move in
the same *direction* as people who see themselves as centre-right, even
if their starting levels of support for particular policies are different.

American researchers found that US public opinion, despite deep party divides, tends to shift in common in a predictable way: towards higher spending preferences under governments that cut spending, and towards cuts under governments that more heavily invest. The public, it seems, is like a thermostat – just as thermostats cut the radiators off when the room temperature rises to a desired level (and put them back on as it falls), so voters move to cut the spending taps off when government grows (and move to turn them back on when it falls).

Britain also has parallel publics. The idea applies to the issues people see as important over time. Not only do different parties' voters tend to move in parallel, their issue priorities are much more similar than we often imagine. When one party's voters think an issue rises in importance, other parties' voters think so too. This can be seen in the figure which tracks the percentages of Conservatives, Labour voters and Lib Dems saying the economy is the most important issue facing the country between 2004 and 2013, and the percentage of people saying immigration is the most important issue.

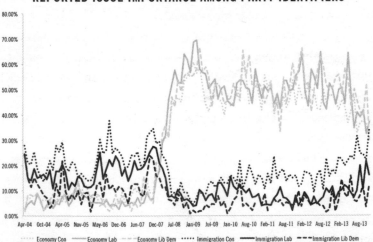

REPORTED ISSUE IMPORTANCE AMONG PARTY IDENTIFIERS

Source: British Election Study Continuing Monitoring Survey

There is hardly any difference in the importance of the economy to Conservatives, Labour voters and Lib Dems. The financial crisis led all three parties' supporters to rate the economy as most important. But perhaps more striking is the similarity between all three groups on immigration. This issue shows barely any difference in reported importance over the ten-year period between 2004 and 2013. These patterns are not unique to the time period in the figure or unique to the economy and immigration. When the issue of immigration rose up the agenda, it rose in importance among Conservatives, Labour voters, Lib Dems and also undecideds. And when Europe was a more important issue to Tories before the 2001 general election, under William Hague, it was also more important to Labour voters, Lib Dems and others. On the flip-side, Labour's focus on the NHS under Blair did not just reflect concern with the NHS among Labour voters alone; health was the most important issue in the early 2000s for Labour voters, Conservatives and Lib Dems alike. Asking about the most important issue facing the country may force people to under-report the importance of other issues, but if different party voters are wedded to particular issue concerns, we should expect some stable differences to exist in issue importance over time. This is not the case.

So, the idea of the party supporter as an unmoving ideologue wedded to certain issue concerns appears to be a caricature. There is more similarity than difference, certainly more than is commonly assumed.

We often think of parties choosing between an appeal to the base and an appeal to the centre ground. The Conservatives were said to be appealing to the core Conservative vote when they campaigned on Europe and immigration in the early 2000s, and on immigration under Howard in 2005. But the finding of parallel publics means that this trade-off is not that clear. Campaigning on a salient issue will appeal – potentially – to a party's own voters and to other voters it hopes to attract. What matters is the broader policy environment which makes some issues salient for all voters, and others less salient. And if a party can raise the importance of an issue by campaigning on that issue and making the political debate about that issue, it may succeed in persuading other party supporters of that issue's importance, too.

When parties do appeal on a narrow issue set, it is more often the case that these are the issues the party is more trusted on – issues the party 'owns', as discussed in the previous chapter – rather than issues only its voters care about. A party's core supporters tend to trust the party on all issues, but the wider electorate will trust a party better on issues it is traditionally associated with. When a party is unpopular, its 'owned issues' may be the only issues on which voters give the party any credibility. Hence parties try to shift the agenda onto issues that benefit them. But this shouldn't be confused with a 'core vote' strategy. Core voters' concerns match the concerns of other parties' voters more closely than you might think.

FURTHER READING

The classic US works on this subject are *The Rational Public: Fifty Years of Trends in Americans' Policy Preferences* by Benjamin I. Page and Robert Y. Shapiro (University of Chicago Press, 1992) and James A. Stimson's *Public Opinion in America: Moods, Cycles, and Swings* (Westview Press, 1991). Data on Britain, and the concept of issue ownership appeals and core voters, comes from 'A Test of Core Vote Theories: The British Conservatives, 1997–2005' (*British Journal of Political Science,* 2011). The idea of public opinion as a thermostat is from Christopher Wlezien's 'The Public as Thermostat: Dynamics of Preferences for Spending' (*American Journal of Political Science,* 1995), and see also the chapter by Will Jennings on this in *Sex, Lies and the Ballot Box* (Biteback, 2014).

—CHAPTER 19—

They only have themselves to blame: immigration and political legitimacy

Lauren McLaren

O pinion polls reveal two clear public views about immigration: there's too much of it, and it is important. The British Social Attitudes surveys indicate, for instance, that over 70 per cent of the public wants immigration reduced. This is nothing new. Surveys from the 1960s reveal similar percentages thinking too many immigrants had already been allowed into the country; this figure rose to 80 per cent by 1970. In the past decade immigration has been consistently ranked as one of the most important issues facing the UK by anything from a third to half of voters.

These widespread concerns about immigration can have electoral consequences – and were a central issue in the EU referendum in 2016 – but they also have a much deeper impact: they affect the fundamental trust voters have in political institutions and leaders. In the past decade, there has been a growing connection between concern about the impact of immigration on the UK and distrust of political institutions and elites in the UK, which suggests that the persistent perception of political failure on immigration is eroding voters' faith in politics.

Voter concern about immigration is old, but the link with political trust is not. Public concern about immigration was not linked to reduced political legitimacy in the 1980s or much of the 1990s. In fact, those most concerned about immigration in the 1980s were slightly more *positive* about the British political system than those who were less concerned. This is presumably because the Conservative Party was in power and was perceived to be stronger at handling immigration than other parties – a perception bolstered by the low and stable migration statistics of the period. Ipsos MORI polls from the late 1970s, for instance, show that 50 per cent of the British public thought the Conservatives had the best policies on immigration, compared to 20 per cent thinking Labour had the best immigration policies. This Conservative lead on immigration continued into the 2000s, but had declined substantially long before the 2010 general election that eventually produced the Conservative–Lib Dem coalition. Throughout much of the 2000s, most people either thought none of the main parties had good immigration policies or couldn't determine which party was best on this issue. Most of the public had lost confidence in the ability of any mainstream political party to address immigration properly (as discussed in Chapter 17). In short, the public once had confidence that government could impact immigration levels – at least under the Conservatives – but that confidence has now been lost.

It is not just political parties that suffer the fallout from this loss of faith, either. Even after accounting for other factors which predict trust such as a person's own prior feelings of distrust, their sense of alienation and their socioeconomic status, concern about immigration is still a powerful predictor of general distrust in politics. Similarly, perceptions of poor policy performance on immigration also contributed to distrust in politics, even taking into account performance across a range of other issues such as the economy, the health service, and crime and terrorism, and extends to distrust in unelected branches of government such as the legal system and the police. The graphs below, for example, show how public concern about immigration, when combined with perceptions that government has handled immigration badly, leads to reduced levels of trust in parliament, politicians and the police. People who think immigrants are not contributing to British culture, for instance, *and* also think the government has not handled immigration well, are significantly less trusting than those who are generally more positive about immigration or satisfied with government performance on the issue.

Parties and party leaders themselves are likely to be at least partly to blame for this, fostering distrust in politics by misleading the public on what can realistically be achieved. Hard-line restrictionist rhetoric does not seem to be believable anymore and is likely to be contributing to the continued demise of trust in politics in the UK.

This is frustrating for political elites, who believe they are trying hard to address public concerns about immigration: both Labour and the Conservatives took many steps to attempt to reduce migration levels, and to ensure that those who stay will integrate into British society. The problem is that these changes did not result in any sustained fall in migration levels, despite promises by both parties that they would. While net migration numbers declined briefly around the time of the 2008 recession, they soon rebounded to record highs. The difficulty of controlling immigration in the modern world is apparent in these numbers, and would have presumably also been clear to any expert on the topic advising the government officials: reducing migration in several large categories of migrants (students, workers) is costly and difficult; in other large migration categories (EU migrants and asylum seekers) it contravenes binding international treaty obligations.

So, in terms of the impact of voters' anxieties about immigration on political trust, a large part of the problem may not necessarily

TRUST IN PARLIAMENT, POLITICIANS AND THE POLICE, BY VIEWS ON IMMIGRATION

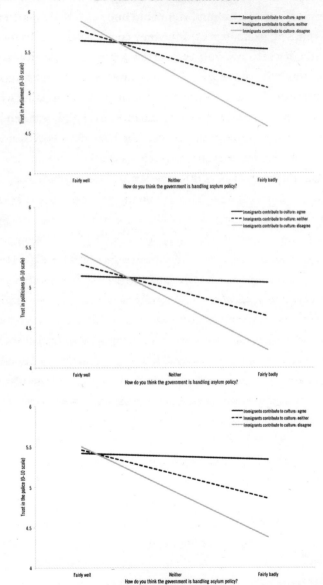

have been the failure to control numbers but instead a political elite that kept promising something – namely big reductions in immigration levels – which it did not, and could not, deliver. The parties, in short, kept setting up expectations they could not meet. Doing this repeatedly harmed not only the parties whose promises failed but trust in the ability of the wider political system as a whole by giving the impression that it was incapable of delivering on an issue which matters for many voters. The consequences of the EU referendum outcome for free movement between the UK and the EU, and for migration in general, remain to be seen – as do the consequences for restoring faith in the UK political system as a whole.

FURTHER READING

The theory and evidence for the connections between immigration, national identity and political trust can be found in Lauren McLaren's *Immigration and Perceptions of National Political Systems in Europe* (Oxford University Press, 2015) and 'Immigration and Perceptions of the Political System in Britain' (*Political Quarterly*, 2013), as well as Jack Citrin et al.'s 'Multicultural Policy and Political Support in European Democracies' (*Comparative Political Studies*, 2014). For a slightly different take on this topic, see Patrick Sturgis et al.'s 'Does Ethnic Diversity Erode Trust?: Putnam's "Hunkering Down" Thesis Reconsidered' (*British Journal of Political Science*, 2011).

—CHAPTER 20—

Neither loved nor trusted: British political parties

Harold Clarke

Writing in the early twentieth century, LSE political scientist and erstwhile Fabian Society activist Graham Wallas famously remarked that political parties were objects that could be 'loved and trusted'. Reliable public opinion surveys were non-existent when Wallas wrote, so there really was no way to determine how widespread positive feelings for parties were at that time. However, if he were observing the political scene today, he very likely would conclude that love and trust for parties are in short supply.

Repeated British Election Study (BES) surveys have documented that psychological identifications with parties have weakened substantially since the 1960s and that many voters lack durable partisan attachments (as discussed in Chapter 6). Surveys also regularly show that many people are not enthusiastic about any of the parties, with overall levels of affection typically ranging from lukewarm to downright chilly.

For example, the average score recorded by the parties on a 0–10 point 'like–dislike' scale in a series of surveys conducted between January 2014 and March 2015 ranged from a high of 4.3 for Labour, to 4.1 for the Conservatives, 3.4 for UKIP and a paltry 3.3 for the

Liberal Democrats. And, although the SNP fared extremely well in the 2015 general election, its average 'like–dislike' score in Scotland was hardly stellar (4.4) either. Plaid Cymru and the Greens recorded mediocre numbers as well.

All of the parties undoubtedly have some enthusiastic fans, but then so too do Colchester United. But – again, just like Colchester United – they fail to generate much broader enthusiasm. Why? Evidence from election studies suggests that the answer is straightforward: parties are assigned major responsibilities in British democracy and many people think that they perform these tasks poorly. Thus, when asked about 'parties generally, not any particular party', many of those participating in national surveys conducted over the past fifteen years express a variety of complaints. As the graph shows, in the May 2015 Essex Continuous Monitoring Survey, fully three-quarters said that there is a big discrepancy between what parties say and what they actually do (an issue discussed further in Chapter 28),

EVALUATING BRITISH POLITICAL PARTIES 2001–2015

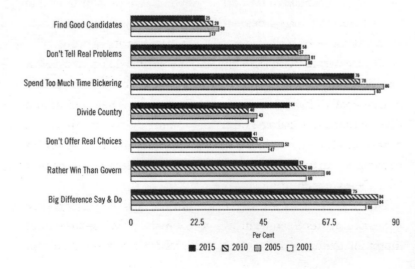

112

with comparable numbers for the 2001, 2005 and 2010 BES surveys ranging as high as 84 per cent. Similarly, large majorities lamented that parties spend too much time bickering and fighting with one another rather than addressing the nation's business. Sizeable majorities also judged that parties do not tell people about the real problems facing the country and are more interested in fighting elections than governing. Large numbers complained parties do more to divide rather than to unite the country, do not offer real choices to the electorate and fail to nominate strong candidates to run for office.

These general adverse reactions to political parties are strongly correlated with negative evaluations in important policy fields such as the economy, the NHS and immigration, as well as negative images of the major party leaders. Populist attitudes were consequential too. Such attitudes are widespread – surveys conducted over the past half-decade regularly document that large majorities believe that contemporary British society is rife with economic inequality, social injustice and corporate greed. As important players in Britain's political–economic establishment, the parties are lightning rods for these populist discontents, and people who endorsed such ideas tended to judge the parties even more harshly. Evaluations of the parties also reflected voters' own characteristics, with feelings of political powerlessness, extreme (both right and left) ideological positions and low levels of social trust also associated with negative party performance judgements. In sum, widespread unhappiness with parties reflects a diverse range of negative evaluations about how Britain's political, economic and social systems are functioning, and accompanying perceptions that 'the system' is rigged and ordinary people cannot have their voices heard.

Do these negative judgements about the general performance of parties matter for the choices voters make or is 'sullen but not mutinous' a more accurate characterisation? Yes, they do. Even after controlling for a broad array of 'usual suspects' in voting behaviour research such as party leader images, partisanship, judgements about the state of the economy and effectiveness in other key policy areas like healthcare and immigration, general judgements about party performance had strong effects on the likelihood of voting for either the Conservatives or Labour versus one of the minor parties in 2015. As general judgements about party performance moved from positive to negative, the probability of voting for the Conservatives or Labour fell markedly – from 89 per cent to only 55 per cent. This big decrease suggests that negative party performance judgements did much to erode major party support in the 2015 election, thereby propelling the surge in minor party voting and the growing fragmentation of the national party system. Reviewing these findings a century after he penned his famous phrase, Wallas might well conclude that a widespread lack of love and trust for British political parties may not be novel, but it can be consequential.

FURTHER READING

Wallas's characterisation of political parties appears in his classic *Human Nature in Politics* (first published in 1908). For evidence concerning modern-day trends in psychological attachments to British parties and individual-level instability in these attachments, see Harold D. Clarke et al.'s *Political Choice in Britain* (Oxford University Press, 2004). Factors affecting voting in the 2015 general election are analysed in *Austerity and Political Choice in Britain* (Palgrave Macmillan, 2015) by Harold D. Clarke et al.

'Public sentiment is everything.
With public sentiment, nothing can fail;
without it nothing can succeed.'

ABRAHAM LINCOLN

—CHAPTER 21—

A growing class divide: MPs and voters

Oliver Heath

The number of women and ethnic minority MPs in Parliament has risen sharply over the last few elections, something which has attracted plenty of media attention. Less notice has been paid to another shift in the social mix of the Commons: the decline in the number of working-class MPs. In 1964, 20 per cent of MPs had a working-class occupational background, but by 2015 just 3 per cent did. This decline is almost entirely due to changes which have occurred within the Labour Party, a party established to ensure working-class representation. In 1964, Labour was not just a party that saw itself as for the working class, but actually was substantially composed of working-class politicians, with 37 per cent of its MPs coming from manual occupational backgrounds. By 2015 this figure had fallen to just 7 per cent. Does this change matter?

Survey evidence collected since 1964 indicates that it does. The decline of working-class MPs within the Labour ranks has substantially reduced the relative popularity of the party among working-class voters, even after controlling for a host of other factors. Working-class people are much more likely than middle-class people to vote Labour when the party contains a substantial number of working-class MPs, and variation over time in the number of working-class Labour MPs closely tracks the strength of such class voting. For example, all other things being equal, the predicted difference between a person from the middle class and the working class voting for Labour is just under forty percentage points if working-class MPs are prominent within the party (at around, say, one third of the total), but this advantage with working-class voters is only twenty-seven percentage points if the working-class MPs are a small minority of Labour's Westminster presence (at around, say, one in ten). Working-class voters also tend to be more likely than the middle class to vote Labour when the local Labour candidate is working class, and working-class voters are more likely to regard Labour as being left-wing when they have a working-class Labour candidate in their constituency.

THE WORKING CLASS ARE MORE LIKELY TO VOTE LABOUR WHEN THERE ARE LOTS OF WORKING-CLASS LABOUR MPS

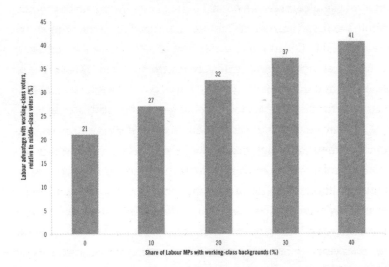

The changes in the occupational background of MPs within the Labour Party are in part the result of a conscious electoral strategy.

Labour selected more and more middle-class candidates to run for office during the 1980s and 1990s as part of an effort to rebrand the party and appeal to middle-class voters put off by Labour's perceived closeness to trade unions and working-class radicalism. The resulting changes in MPs' occupational background have made Parliament less representative of the broader British population, and the Labour Party much less representative of the working class whose interests it was traditionally supposed to champion. The main parties have also become less socially distinct from each other – and in the eyes of many voters now resemble rival middle-class 'management teams'.

While experiments varying prospective MPs' backgrounds reveal everyone is put off by very wealthy candidates, it is people from a working-class background who are particularly repelled, especially when it comes to judging how approachable candidates are. MPs from privileged backgrounds are indeed perceived as less 'in touch' by working-class voters, who will regard a pledge to stand up for the underprivileged as more credible coming from someone whose own background is modest than a similar promise coming from the child of millionaires. By extension, a party which contains many working-class MPs will be seen by working-class voters as more likely to effectively stand up for their interests.

Over time, the two parties have become ideologically more similar, but they have also become socially more similar, and it is this social similarity that appears to have the strongest impact on class voting. Although the loss of working-class MPs has not hurt Labour electorally overall – and may even have paid off in terms of making them more appealing to many middle-class voters, at least during the Blair years – it has come at the cost of participatory equality. As the Labour Party has become more middle-class, working-class people have become less likely to vote at all.

According to the British Election Study, in 2010 the difference in reported turnout between the working class and the middle class was nineteen percentage points, compared to less than just five percentage points in 1964. To give a comparison, in 2010 the difference in reported turnout between the under-thirties and the over-sixties – one of the turnout differentials that most excites people – was twenty-one percentage points.

Indeed, by 2010 the impact of class on turnout was greater than the impact of class on vote choice. For the first time since the introduction of the mass franchise, class was more important as a participatory divide than it was as an electoral divide. This represents an important milestone in British political history. Traditionally Britain was regarded as *the* class society, where class was pre-eminent among the factors used to explain party allegiance. In comparative terms, the impact of class on vote in Britain has long been unusually high – and was one way in which Britain stood apart from the USA, where class did not divide the parties, but did divide voters from non-voters. The middle-class-focused centrism which Tony Blair learned from Bill Clinton made Britain more like America in an unexpected way: working-class voters have responded here, as they did in the US, by turning their backs on the electoral process altogether.

FURTHER READING

For a more detailed discussion of the findings discussed here, see Oliver Heath's 'Policy Representation, Social Representation, and Class Voting in Britain' (*British Journal of Political Science*, 2015). The survey experiments are discussed in Rosie Campbell and Philip Cowley's 'Rich Man, Poor Man, Politician Man: Wealth Effects in a Candidate Biography Survey Experiment' (*British Journal of Politics and International Relations*, 2014). Robert Ford and Matthew Goodwin's *Revolt on the Right: Explaining Support for the Radical Right in Britain* (Routledge, 2014) provides a wide-ranging account of how the working class have become disillusioned with the political class in general.

CHAPTER 22

When do women vote for women?
The role of gender ideology

Rosie Campbell

When women candidates began to stand for Parliament in larger numbers, one concern was whether sexist voters would react negatively and punish them at the ballot box. Such effects as did exist were always pretty minor and have long since vanished, and there is now no evidence that women candidates perform differently to men when they stand for office in Britain.

Instead, attention has shifted to a different issue: whether women might actually prefer to have women representatives, and be more likely to vote for women candidates.

There was little international evidence that women behave like this – with one notable exception. The 1992 congressional elections in the US became known as 'the year of the woman', both due to the unprecedented number of women elected to the Senate and because of a public debate about gender equality resulting from the confirmation of Clarence Thomas as a Supreme Court justice despite accusations of sexual harassment. Women voters in the US responded to the unusual salience of gender in politics, showing a preference for women candidates that year – although only when the woman candidate was viewed as feminist.

In the UK, there has similarly been little evidence of women systematically voting for women. Although research has shown that women would like to see more women MPs in the House of Commons, they were as an overall group not particularly concerned about the sex of their own MP. However, women are a very large and diverse group – more than half of the electorate – and so while women overall may not vote for women, perhaps some groups of women do respond to the sex of their local candidates.

The 2010 British election provided a good opportunity to test this idea, both because the availability of women candidates, in a range of constituencies and parties, was much higher than in previous years, and because the issue of women's political representation was more salient than in preceding elections, largely as a result of the intra-party debate about all-women shortlists – a debate which was present to a greater or lesser extent in all three major parties.

As before, there was no systematic evidence of women voting disproportionately for women candidates in 2010. But when we look a little closer, we find that *some* women did vote for women. Just as in the US in 1992, what mattered in Britain in 2010 was not biological sex, but gender ideology. Women with feminist views were more likely to choose women candidates – because their gender ideology is congruent with the view that women should be actively involved in politics and public life. In short, the women who view gender equality as an important political goal vote accordingly.

In broad terms, gender ideology has two poles, from traditional (a woman's place is in the home, and so on) to feminist (women should have a role in public life equal to that of men).

One way to measure gender ideology is by combining responses to the following two statements about gender equality, from the 2010 British Election Study:

1. Women are better representatives of women's interests than men
2. Women need to get more involved in politics to solve problems that concern them

Overall, women were more likely to agree with both statements than men, particularly the second, where 67 per cent of women agreed with the statement compared to 53 per cent of men. Combining the responses to both statements we can create a scale to capture the intensity of a voter's feminist ideology (ranging from 0 for a traditional gender ideology to 8 for a feminist gender ideology). There is a very small but important difference between men and women, with women being slightly more feminist on average than men.

And whereas biological sex did not help predict whether women will vote for women candidates, how voters responded to these statements about gender equality did have an impact on whether women voted for women candidates, but no impact on men's decision making. For women with the highest scores of eight on the feminism scale, the chances of voting for a party were 1.6 times higher if it put forward a woman candidate than a male candidate. This means that about three strongly feminist women voted for a party when it put forward a woman candidate for every two women who voted for that party when it put forward a man. Those who really care about the representation of women were much more likely to respond when a party put forward a woman candidate than women who did not really care about the issue.

However, only a small share of the female electorate have such strong feminist views; of the 942 women who completed these survey questions just 28 – or 3 per cent – had the maximum score of 8. And even among feminist women relatively few were prepared to compromise on their preferred party simply due to the sex of the candidate.

This group of feminist women is a small section of the voting-age population and get lost in broader analysis of voting. And because they are small, they are unlikely to drive the political parties to select women candidates in order to secure votes.

So, when parties attempt to improve the representation of women they are not doing this for electoral advantage in individual seats. Standing more women candidates will secure some votes from feminist women in those particular constituencies, but not enough to make much of a difference. Instead, such action is part of a broader strategy to present a modern party image to all voters.

FURTHER READING

The US research on 'the year of the woman' can be found in Kathleen Dolan's 'Voting for Women in the "Year of the Woman"' (*American Journal of Political Science*, 1998) and Eric Plutzer and John Zipp's 'Identity Politics, Partisanship, and Voting for Women Candidates' (*Public Opinion Quarterly*, 1996). For attitudes towards the representation of women and other groups, see Philip Cowley's 'Why Not Ask the Audience? Understanding the Public's Representational Priorities' (*British Politics*, 2013). And for the findings on the 2010 election, see 'Do Women Vote for Women Candidates? Attitudes towards Descriptive Representation and Voting Behaviour in the 2010 British Election' (*Politics and Gender*, forthcoming), by Rosie Campbell and Oliver Heath.

—CHAPTER 23—

Effective but unpopular?
Gender quotas

David Cutts

Women parliamentarians outnumber men in only two countries. While Rwanda and Bolivia top the list, elsewhere across the world the proportion of women in lower or single houses of parliament also now exceeds 30 per cent in nearly fifty countries. Almost twenty-five years ago, Argentina became the first country in the world to pass a gender quota law requiring parties to nominate specific percentages of women to the legislature. Now more than 120 countries have adopted one or more types of gender quota. Of the top twenty countries with the highest number of women parliamentarians, only five do not have any kind of gender quota in place.

But in some countries the implementation of quotas has coincided with informal practices of subversion. Party elites have frequently used a wide range of tactics from placing women in unelectable positions on party lists to nominating the spouses or girlfriends of male party officials (known in Mexico as 'Juanitas') to fill the quota while simultaneously registering their husbands or boyfriends as substitutes. After the election they get the women to renounce their seats, allowing their male counterparts to enter the legislature. Elsewhere, to evade quota laws, parties have gone so far as to put up fake candidates, often placing male candidates on lists under female names. Such tactics have often backfired with electoral rules tightened, laws enforced and even quota limits being raised. But if quotas are so effective and useful, as the evidence suggests, this prompts some important questions: why do party elites go to such extremes to subvert them? And why do voters in many countries seem unconvinced by their merits?

There are numerous objections to gender quotas. Many argue they undermine selection on merit; that quota candidates are less qualified and face an easier path to selection; and that quotas end up only benefiting elite women, and so don't actually improve the representation of the truly marginalised. There are also claims that voters penalise quota candidates at the ballot box and that they are regarded by fellow parliamentarians as somehow 'second class', who leave elected office early and often fail to reach top legislative or executive positions.

Numerous comparative studies of male and female parliamentarians have found little basis for any of these objections. Women elected by quotas are equally qualified or in some countries more qualified than their male or non-quota colleagues. Evidence from Sweden even suggests that the use of quotas has increased male competition, leading to better qualified male candidates too. Other studies have found that women elected by quotas are as or more productive in legislatures, that they have profiles no different from non-quota counterparts, and that the quota label doesn't have any bearing on legislative or executive careers.

Arguments about the negative electoral impact of gender quotas became prominent in Britain following the election of the independent candidate Peter Law in the historically Labour safe seat of Blaenau Gwent in the 2005 general election. Law was opposed to Labour's use of an all-women shortlist (AWS) in the seat. 'This is what happens when you don't listen,' he proclaimed, as he overturned a 17,000 Labour majority. But the electoral earthquake in Blaenau Gwent only proved to be a minor tremor and was not representative. Studies examining each general election where AWS has been used show that the rebellion in the Welsh valleys was a one-off: candidates selected on AWS (who are by definition new candidates) do on average about as well as new candidates selected by other methods, if slightly worse than incumbents who have the advantage of profile and experience. Other studies have found that quotas can change female perceptions of and engagement with the system. Women become more likely to participate in politics when women candidates stand for election, party elites become less biased against women and political cultures become less sexist.

In India, following an amendment to the constitution in the early 1990s, gender quotas through reserved seats for women were randomly assigned to village councils across a series of elections. Multiple academic studies have taken advantage of this natural experiment and provide clear evidence that these randomly assigned gender quotas affected overall perceptions of women's political competence in a positive way. Women also become more confident in the ability of women to govern when they see more women in their national legislature. And more recently, a study of nearly fifty countries found clear evidence that gender quotas positively affect individual attitudes to women as political leaders, and that this differs by sex, a phenomenon referred to as a 'vote of confidence' effect.

But despite their merits, gender quotas remain contentious. A recent YouGov poll in Britain found that 56 per cent did not support the use of AWS, with opposition strongest among men, those over sixty and among Conservative and UKIP voters. Even among Labour voters, more oppose than support AWS. And when asked to rank which measures would be the most effective way to elect more women MPs, only 4 per cent of Britons chose imposing gender quotas. A majority favoured either more education or training for women to encourage them to stand for office or placed the onus on political institutions to make politics more family friendly. Across twenty-seven European countries, a similar question evoked more confidence in gender quotas, but still only 18 per cent of European citizens ranked it as the most effective solution.

Most surveys in Britain find that a majority of Britons agree that women are underrepresented in Parliament. Most advocate more women in politics. A healthy number agree that women parliamentarians best represent women's interests. Across the globe there is striking evidence that quotas have had a substantial impact on the numbers of women elected to legislatures. Even in Britain, AWS has been the main driver of increasing numbers of women entering the House of Commons. Yet despite their undoubted effectiveness at fostering positive outcomes, gender quotas overwhelmingly lack public backing and in a number of quarters remain despised. Sometimes public opinion is a muddled beast.

FURTHER READING

A detailed insight into the different types of quotas used worldwide and their impact can be found in *The Impact of Gender Quotas* edited by Susan Franceschet et al. (Oxford University Press, 2012). For the Indian experimental evidence on the impact of gender quotas, see Lori Beaman et al.'s 'Female Leadership Raises Aspirations and Educational Attainment for Girls: A Policy Experiment in India' (*Science*, 2012). For British literature, see 'Measuring the Quality of Politicians Elected by Gender Quotas – Are They Any Different?', by Peter Allen et al. (*Political Studies*, 2014) or '"This Is What Happens When You Don't Listen": All-Women Shortlists at the 2005 General Election' (*Party Politics*, 2008) by David Cutts et al.

CHAPTER 24

Neither Arthur nor Martha: gender identities

Nicola Wildash

G ender is an essential demographic within all surveys and is fundamental to social research. Most (if not all) research companies ask the question as follows:

Are you male or female?
1. Male
2. Female

It's a binary, forced choice, question. All respondents are expected to know this information, and it allows pollsters to match up this demographic to official data (from the Office of National Statistics), increasing the representativeness of their samples and the accuracy and reliability of data.

Recently, YouGov were approached by the Nonbinary Inclusion Project to discuss this standard gender question. This grassroots organisation is fighting for the inclusion and recognition of non-binary people in law, media and everyday life, and wanted to understand how the market research industry approach the issue of gender. It is an issue which is being discussed more than ever before with companies and institutions making changes as a response. OkCupid and Facebook, for example, now offer gender identities other than male and female.

For statistical purposes, YouGov – like other pollsters – continue to use the binary question, but discussions with this organisation led the company to want to explore the question of how straightforward gender actually is.

YouGov had previously examined sexuality as a scale (finding that 19 per cent of the public don't classify themselves as 100 per cent heterosexual or homosexual but somewhere in between) and wondered if a similar scale exists for gender. To investigate, we contacted a nationally representative study of over 14,000 British adults and asked them to place themselves on a numeric scale where 0 was female and 100 was male.

While most people placed themselves at the far ends of the scale, there were many who did not – more than we had expected. Our assumption was that a small number of respondents might not identify as male or female (and place themselves along the scale) but the overall picture would be that most women would describe themselves as 100 per cent female and most men as 100 per cent male.

We firstly grouped all women who said 0 and all men who said 100 into group 1 (representing those who see their gender as 100 per cent male or female). Women who gave an answer between 1 and 5 and men who gave an answer between 95 and 99 were placed into group 2 or 'Strong'. The final group (group 3) included everyone who placed themselves anywhere else on the scale (between 6 and 94). For our initial analysis, we removed anyone who placed themselves on the opposite side of the scale to what was expected in case these answers were given by mistake, for example a man who gave an answer of 0. We also removed the 281 people (44 per cent men and 56 per cent women) who answered 'not sure'.

The results showed that almost half of men (48 per cent) see themselves at the extreme end of the gender scale compared with only 7 per cent of women. Over two thirds of women identified strongly but not completely as a female. The majority of people identify with one gender or another, but women are less likely to state themselves as being 100 per cent female.

To investigate this difference further, we repeated the experiment in other countries in Europe to see whether or not this pattern only applied in Britain. We contacted representative samples of over 1,000 adults in France, Germany, Denmark and Sweden. As the table shows, the pattern was mirrored among all the countries we looked at, with men more likely than women to perceive themselves as 100 per cent their gender.

Women in all five countries were more likely to appear in group 2 than in group 1. Only 4 per cent of women in Germany and 5 per cent of women in France placed themselves at the extreme end of the scale. There was more variety in the groups German men appeared in compared with Britain, with 51 per cent of British men not answering 100, compared with almost 70 per cent of German men.

PERCENTAGE OF MEN AND WOMEN IN EACH GENDER IDENTITY GROUP

Gender identity group	BRITAIN		GERMANY		FRANCE		DENMARK		SWEDEN	
	Male	Female	Male	Female	Male	Female	Male	Female	Male	Female
100% (1)	48	7	32	4	32	5	47	7	45	7
Strong (2)	32	70	36	65	32	56	32	65	28	61
Weak (3)	19	23	31	31	36	39	21	29	27	33

So what is causing this? Perhaps the scale was too difficult for some to understand or complete, but unless we are going to entertain the notion that women don't understand scales and men do, that doesn't offer an explanation for the sex differences we find.

What could be happening, though, is that men and women *perceive* the question in different ways. The question 'Where would you place yourself on the following scale?', although simple, leaves much to the eye of the beholder. Perhaps men are seeing this as a purely biological question, resulting in larger numbers of them choosing 100 per cent male as their answer. In contrast, women might be thinking of their biology combined with personality and character traits, resulting in a higher number of women placing themselves away from the extreme end of the scale.

The group of respondents who placed themselves on the opposite side of the scale to what we expected also reinforces this argument: ninety-nine men placed themselves on the female half of the scale while 181 women placed themselves on the male side. We assume that those (three men and thirty-six women) who put themselves at the furthest point on the opposite side may have answered in error. However, almost 50 per cent more women than men placed themselves on the opposite side of the scale, which could further illustrate that women were answering the question differently to men – choosing to answer in terms of personality rather than biology and revealing a sort of 'tomboy effect'.

This data may also be an illustration of modern day masculinity. It is not illogical to argue that men are more uncomfortable with the idea that they are not 100 per cent male and therefore see the extreme value as the obvious answer to give. It is not that men are wrongly identifying themselves as male, but that they want to say they are *100 per cent* male. This also appears to be the case when comparing age groups. Older generations are less likely to place themselves away from the extreme ends of the scale (in Britain a third of 18–24-year-olds were in group 3 compared with just 15 per cent of over-sixties), supporting this idea that different people will perceive the question differently – and that gender is not so straightforward after all.

FURTHER READING

For work on gender and sexuality generally, see Judith Butler's book *Undoing Gender* (Routledge, 2004). For thoughts on modern masculinities and femininities see *Gender, Culture and Society: Contemporary Femininities and Masculinities* by Máirtin Mac an Ghaill and Chris Haywood (Palgrave Macmillan, 2007) or 'Re-examining Masculinity, Femininity, and Gender Identity Scales' by Kay M. Palan, Charles S. Areni and Pamela Kiecker (*Marketing Letters*, 1999). For sociological approaches to understanding how and why social work is arranged around gender distinctions, see Mary Holmes's book *What is Gender? Sociological Approaches* (Sage, 2007).

CHAPTER 25

Immigration or visibility? Ethnic minority representation

Maria Sobolewska

As we celebrate the huge increases in presence of ethnic minorities in Westminster in 2010 and 2015, it is easy to forget that the new cohort of minority MPs still represents a significant shortfall in terms of reflecting the wider population. While there are many theories as to why this underrepresentation occurs, we still lack a clear explanation, largely because even though the ethnic minority population is different in many respects from other underrepresented groups such as women, gay or disabled people, we often discuss these different forms of underrepresentation together, and as a result we try to fit the same explanatory narratives to very different cases.

Yet there is one case more directly comparable to that of ethnic minorities: other immigrants. Most ethnic minorities are still of fairly recent immigrant origin, so one obvious yet curiously unexplored explanation for their underrepresentation could be just this: the experience of immigration. This could be an obstacle to all immigrants, whatever their origin, but it should disappear once further generations grow up in Britain. However, the other factors associated with being from an ethnically distinct group, such as racial discrimination, will not be equally distributed across immigrants and may be more persistent in second and even third generations.

When we draw this distinction, we find that immigration itself is indeed an obstacle to representation, but visibility poses an additional challenge – albeit one that has been diminishing over time.

There are many reasons why people who immigrate into a new country face disadvantages in joining that country's political elite: such as a lack of country-specific political knowledge, lower interest in that country's politics or isolation from the social networks in the host country. Although in the case of Britain those who arrived from any of the countries of the Commonwealth and Ireland are able to participate fully in politics upon arrival, generally immigrants' eligibility to vote and to stand in national elections is only awarded with citizenship, which takes time and forms another important obstacle for representation.

By tracking down all the first- and second-generation immigrants who have sat in the House of Commons, including those who had only one parent migrate into the UK, we can build a clearer picture of the political impact of migrant status. Within these immigrant-origin MPs, we can further distinguish between those usually classified as ethnic minority (black and Asian) and those of white immigrant origins. And then within the white group we can also identify those who are seemingly of immigrant origin due to their foreign-sounding names.

When we take this broader approach to representation, we discover, first, that the UK does relatively well in representing immigrants. Out of eight European countries studied, Britain is second only to Holland in the proportion of immigrant-origin MPs serving in the national legislature.

But second, when we compare the percentages of those MPs who were of immigrant origin but were born in the UK to one or both immigrant parents with those who immigrated themselves, it becomes clear that the experience of immigration does indeed impede representation. Although in 2010 11 per cent of all MPs were of immigrant origin, only 3 per cent were immigrants themselves. It is hard to be sure whether this represents a good match with population proportions, as the Office of National Statistics (ONS) does not publish up-to-date data on second-generation immigrants, but in 2011 the ONS estimated that 14 per cent of the British population were immigrants, and thus 3 per cent represents a sizeable representation shortfall.

The next step is to consider whether the visibility of immigrant background (on the basis of skin colour or name) is a further obstacle to representation. This is trickier than it sounds, since we have – as previously indicated – trouble establishing how many Britons are of immigrant origin in general. It is even harder to track the representation of individual groups of immigrants. However, looking at the 2011 Census we see that while only 4.5 per cent of the UK's residents identified as non-British white, as many as 14 per cent identified as belonging to an ethnic minority. This is likely an underestimation of the non-British white groups, as the second-generation children of, for example, a white American parent (such as Winston Churchill) may be more likely to identify as white British, but they would still be coded as immigrant-origin MPs. Thus, while we know for sure that ethnic minorities in Britain remain underrepresented, and by how much, we do not have a comparable figure for the white immigrant groups.

But looking at the figure (below), we can see two trends: first there is an increasing number of MPs of all immigrant backgrounds, and second there is a closing of the gap between the numbers of MPs of visible and invisible immigrant origin. While in 2001 MPs with visibly 'foreign' backgrounds were just over a third of all immigrant-origin MPs, by 2010 they were almost a half of all those MPs.

PERCENTAGE OF WESTMINSTER MPS OF
VISIBLE AND INVISIBLE IMMIGRANT ORIGIN

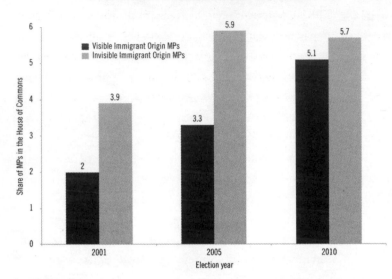

Source: Pathways data

This is at least a major step in the right direction. As the prejudice against new groups weakens and they acquire more resources to enable them to integrate politically, parity of representation now seems a realistic proposition. However, the experience of immigration, one that affects only the immigrants themselves and not their children, will remain an obstacle to representation, and with the share of migrants in Britain steadily rising, this is perhaps a problem that now deserves our attention.

FURTHER READING

To read more about the political representation of ethnic minorities in Britain see 'Party Strategies, Political Opportunity Structure and the Descriptive Representation of Ethnic Minorities in Britain' by Maria Sobolewska (*West European Politics*, 2013) and for how visible difference can be an obstacle read '"Acceptable Difference": Diversity, Representation and Pathways to UK Politics' (*Parliamentary Affairs*, 2013) by Catherine Durose and others. This chapter draws on the Pathways study, the first to go beyond black and Asian minorities' representation and collect data on all immigrant-origin politicians. More information on the project can be found at www.pathways.eu. The British part of the project has been funded by the ESRC and the data has been collected by Patrick English from Manchester University.

'Mothers may still want their favorite sons
to grow up to be President, but ... they do not want
them to become politicians in the process.'

JOHN FITZGERALD KENNEDY

CHAPTER 26

Worse than estate agents: the problem of political trust

Ben Seyd

A measure of the low regard in which people in Britain hold political actors is that politicians are trusted even less than estate agents. An Ipsos MORI poll conducted in December 2015 found just 21 per cent of people trusted politicians while 25 per cent said they trusted estate agents. And people's attitudes to politicians seem to have hardened over time. Thirty years ago, the British Social Attitudes survey found that 40 per cent of the population was at least moderately trusting in government; by 2013, that figure had more than halved to 17 per cent.

These figures are fairly familiar and suggest British people today are not only discontented with their politicians but are markedly more so now than they used to be. One frequently cited reason for this contemporary discontent lies in cases of political misconduct or sleaze such as the Cash for Questions affair (in 1994), the fall-out over the Iraq war (in 2003) and the MPs' expenses scandal (in 2009). Thanks to increasingly inquisitive newspapers and the spread of information via social media, it is argued, we now know far more about what politicians get up to, and much of this is not pretty.

If this was all there was to citizen discontent, we could at least chart a route towards a more contented and trusting population. As long as politicians kept their hands out of the till and were more open and honest in explaining their decisions (admittedly both big asks), citizens would take a more positive view of their elected representatives. Yet two perspectives – one from history and the second from psychology – suggest that things may not be this simple. History suggests that public discontent is by no means new. Popular distrust may have risen as a result of recent political scandals, but a lot of citizens have been grumpy about their politicians for a long time. Take, for example, a Gallup poll which found that people were as likely to believe that politicians were out for themselves as believed they were motivated by the good of the country. The date of this poll? 1944. Even if people have become less trusting recently, popular discontent with politicians is a long-standing feature, not a recent one. If half the country distrusted Churchill and colleagues at the time of the Normandy landings, what hope do today's politicians have?

The psychological perspective helps us to understand why negativity towards politicians is so prevalent and persistent. People tend to weigh negative information more heavily than the positive and take more notice of information that conveys potential harm than that which conveys potential benefit. Neurological studies show that images of untrustworthy faces generate a stronger response within the human brain than those of trustworthy faces. Outside the laboratory, studies have shown how people's reactions to public officials are more strongly shaped by negative engagements with these officials than positive ones. Negative encounters with the police, for example, reduce public confidence much more than positive encounters increase it.

The nation's politicians face a similar problem. People's evaluations of political leaders are affected more by negative assessments of the way they do their job than by positive assessments. We can see this in the way that negative feelings (anger, disgust, unease, fear) about the economy, the NHS and immigration are more strongly associated with distrust of politicians than are positive feelings (happiness, hope, confidence, pride) are with trust. The figure below shows that, while 38 per cent of people who feel positively about the economy also trust politicians, rather more people (59 per cent) who feel negatively about the economy distrust politicians. When it comes to the NHS and immigration, negative feelings again stimulate distrust more than positive feelings stimulate trust.

HOW POSITIVE AND NEGATIVE EVALUATIONS AFFECT TRUST IN POLITICIANS

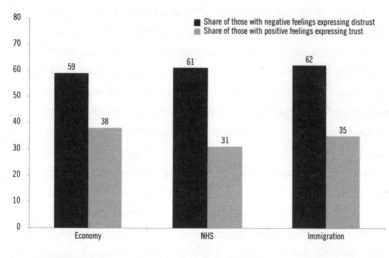

Source: British Election Study 2010

Thus, even if people are exposed to an equal balance of positive and negative news about politicians, this 'negativity bias' means that the latter will have a stronger effect on perceptions of politicians. And given the negative tone and content of so much of today's media reporting of politics, even an equal balance between negative and positive stories may be hard to come by.

A second psychological feature which may perpetuate popular discontent with politicians is the tendency to interpret new information in ways that fit existing beliefs. People hold all sorts of values and beliefs. When they encounter new information that is consistent with these, they readily accept that information. But when they encounter information that is inconsistent with their beliefs, they usually find a way to explain it away. This 'confirmation bias' has been found to affect people's receptiveness to new information on issues like nuclear power and genetically modified food. It also affects their views of political personnel. If people already hold a dim view of politicians (as most do), they will be prone to discount information about politicians' achievements and successes and more ready to accept information about their failures and follies.

These basic psychological principles help explain why citizen distrust of politicians is so widespread and stubbornly persistent. Faced with figures in authority, evolutionary stimuli predispose people to focus on their negative features rather than on their positive ones. Once people have adopted a distrustful attitude, it becomes difficult for new information to move them on from this mindset, since negative information is readily accepted while positive information is wished away.

Yet do these historical and psychological perspectives suggest that people will always be discontented with their politicians? Probably not. If people were psychologically programmed to distrust people in authority, we should find popular scepticism not only of politicians but also of figures like judges and the police. Yet the latest Ipsos MORI poll shows high levels of trust in these groups, with 80 per cent of British people trusting the former and 68 per cent trusting the latter. A psychological explanation for distrust would also suggest that people in different countries should be similarly sceptical of their politicians. Yet 60 per cent of people in Finland and 55 per cent of people in Denmark trust their governments, according to the latest Eurobarometer survey. Judges in Britain and politicians in Finland appear to be doing something right. It is possible that British politicians could do the same. But a glance at history and psychology suggests it will not be easy.

FURTHER READING

A historical perspective on people's attitudes to politicians in Britain is provided by Kevin Jefferys in his *Politics and the People: A History of British Democracy since 1918* (Atlantic, 2007). The impact of psychological processes on trust is introduced in Paul Slovic's 'Perceived Risk, Trust and Democracy', in *Social Trust and the Management of Risk* (Earthscan, 1999). On people's 'negativity bias' in political judgements, see Stuart N. Soroka's *Negativity in Democratic Politics* (Cambridge University Press, 2014).

—CHAPTER 27—

Not love, actually: the public and their MPs

Philip Cowley

In 1975, the political scientist Dick Fenno noted how the US Congress was tremendously unpopular as an institution, yet at the same time its individual members were both popular with their constituents and routinely re-elected. With the originality for which academics are renowned, this effect – often popularised as Why We Hate Congress but Love Our Congressman – became known as Fenno's paradox.

Spend any time around Westminster and you'll hear a variant of Fenno's paradox. Everyone knows that people don't much like MPs, but there is an often-repeated caveat: while people don't like MPs *as a species*, they often quite like *their* MP. For politicians this is a bit of a comfort blanket; after years of press and public hostility, they can reassure themselves that the animosity is nothing personal, that while politicians may be disliked, they personally are OK.

A dig into the data, though, suggests the comfort blanket is a lot thinner than MPs might like.

For example, in late 2014 the British Election Study (BES) asked respondents how much trust they had in MPs 'in general' and how much they had in the MP 'in your local constituency'. Responses were on a seven-point scale, from 1 (no trust) to 7 (a lot of trust).

Over half of respondents had low levels of trust in MPs overall (that is, a response of 1 to 3), and just 20 per cent had high levels of trust (5 to 7). That's a net score (high trust minus low trust) of -36. The equivalent net score for trust in their local MP was -6. That's significantly better, but it is still negative. Even when it comes to their own MP, then, we are still talking about just a third of respondents who said that they trusted them – and more who distrusted their local elected representative than trusted them.

And while these general and local responses are not identical, they are not fully independent either. If we calculate the *relative* trust respondents have in politicians (that is, the score for MPs in general minus the score for local MPs), there are more people who trust their local MP more than MPs in general (46 per cent) than the other way around (17 per cent), but almost as many (38 per cent) trusted (or distrusted) the two groups exactly the same. And the differences really are not all that great: given a range of relative scores from -6 to +6, a full 67 per cent gave an answer that was either identical or at most a point different to both questions.

So when we say that 'people' are more positive about their MP than MPs in general, we are talking about a minority of people (albeit a minority sizeable enough to shift aggregate scores), most of whom are only slightly more positive. Given the way the issue is often discussed, you might expect some people to be very negative about MPs but very positive about their own MP. But out of 24,000 respondents to the BES, just 101 gave a score of 1 for MPs but 7 for their MP. That's 0.4%. There are, in other words, vanishingly few people who 'hate' MPs in general but 'love' their local representative.

One of the biggest determinants of whether you trust your MP is whether they are from the same party that you support. You see this clearly in the graph, which shows the trust respondents had in their local MP, broken down both by the party of the MP and then by whether the respondent was a supporter of that party or not. For each of what were then the three main parties, trust in MPs from supporters was signifi- cantly higher than trust from opponents. Perhaps this shouldn't be a huge surprise. If you share the views and political prejudices of your MP, you'll likely trust them more than if you don't. Plus, partisanship colours lots of things (for examples see Chapters 16 and 39), and this isn't any different.

But it is a reminder that trust in politicians isn't like trust in your local GP or your local bus service or in a supermarket. It's a *political* judgement, one driven as much by the views of respondents as by the performance of the MPs.

This helps explain why most local MPs do so badly on this meas- ure – because in most seats in the UK (unlike in most in the US) the majority of constituents didn't vote for the winning candidate.

TRUST IN YOUR MP, BY PARTY AND VOTE, 2014

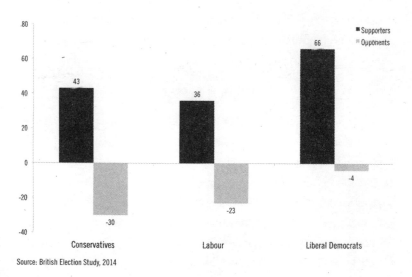

Source: British Election Study, 2014

In the 2015 general election, for example, the winning candidate polled less than half of votes in 51 per cent of constituencies – and even in most of the other 49 per cent there were significant minorities who didn't vote for them. Dissatisfaction is therefore built into the system. It probably also explains why MPs overestimate how popular they are locally – because they probably talk more to supporters than opponents, and among that group they are indeed well trusted.

In passing, it's worth noting that the Lib Dems did better among *both* supporters and opponents, and a lot of Lib Dem MPs hoped that this extra trust would save them in the 2015 election. Spoiler alert: it didn't.

So, the idea that we really rate our local MP while hating MPs in general is wide of the mark. Most people rate their local MP pretty much the same as they rate MPs in general, and a minority are a bit more positive about their local MP than they are about MPs in general. This isn't half as snappy, but it's much closer to the truth. Whatever it is that the British feel about their own MP, it is most definitely not love. To adapt a quote often attributed to Harry Truman (but, like most half-decent political quotes, probably never said by the person to whom it is attributed): any MPs who want love should buy a spaniel.

FURTHER READING

Fenno first noted this effect in 'If, as Ralph Nader Says, Congress Is "the Broken Branch", How Come We Love Our Congressmen So Much?' in *Congress in Change* (Praeger, 1975). His *Home Style* (Longman, 1978) is also excellent on how politicians in the US build and maintain support locally. The single best account of the rise of the local face of British politicians remains Philip Norton and David M. Wood's *Back from Westminster* (University Press of Kentucky, 1993). On the differing meanings of political trust, see 'Does One Trust Judgement Fit All? Linking Theory and Empirics' (*British Journal of Politics and International Relations*, 2010), by Justin Fisher et al.

—CHAPTER 28—

Worth the paper they're written on: party manifestos

Nicholas Allen

Ahead of the 2015 British general election, Labour leader Ed Miliband unveiled a giant limestone slab on which were engraved six key pledges. Had Labour won the election, the widely lampooned 'Ed Stone' was to have served as an unavoidable reminder of the party's commitments. Yet Miliband's accompanying promise to 'restore faith in politics by delivering what we promised at this general election' was doomed to fail. The irony is that even if Labour had delivered on the Ed Stone pledges in full, most voters probably wouldn't have believed it.

Most voters just take it for granted that governments renege on their election manifesto commitments. They suspect that politicians will say almost anything to get elected, including making promises they know they cannot keep. In survey after survey, only small minorities of voters say that parties do what they say they will.

Yet like so much conventional wisdom, popular beliefs about election pledges are mostly wrong. Winning parties do implement the bulk of their manifesto promises. Research suggests that since 1945 British governments that held office for at least four years tended to fulfil around four-fifths of their manifesto pledges. That they did so is less surprising than it might appear. Manifestos are bound up with ideas about mandates: a government's right to implement its policies is coupled with a perceived responsibility to do so. Between elections, political parties usually devote a great deal of time and energy to policy-review exercises, which tend to filter out impossible commitments. Once elected, ministers face consistent pressure from within their party to deliver. They also face pressure from outside. It doesn't matter if voters didn't read or don't remember past manifesto pledges; journalists and opponents do – and will soon remind voters if the government fails to fulfil them.

Of course, all governments fail to do some of the things they said they would, and also end up doing things they said they would not do. Sometimes circumstances require parties to rethink their plans. In its 2005 manifesto, Labour promised not to raise the top rate of income tax until at least after the next election. After the 2008 financial crisis, it felt it had to do just that. The Liberal Democrats pledged in 2010 to 'scrap unfair university tuition fees'. As part of the give and take of being in coalition, the party's leadership felt obliged to vote in favour of allowing fees to rise from £3,000 to £9,000.

Expecting politicians to stick to all prior promises would make politics impossible and bad government more likely. Manifestos represent parties' medium-term policy priorities. They are wide-ranging blueprints for government, but much of the policy detail can only be worked out when in office, and some rethinking of priorities is inevitable as governments are confronted with limited resources and the problems of implementation. For these reasons, most manifesto pledges tend to be relatively general. According to one study, only 40 per cent of pledges in winning-party manifestos between 1945 and 2001 were of the specific or detailed variety.

Indeed, this is one of the reasons why there is this clash between the public's perception that parties regularly renege on their promises and academics' belief that they tend to keep them. Researchers tend to focus on matching winning parties' activity to specific manifesto commitments where it is possible to make objective judgements as to whether or not an action was taken or a goal achieved. They exclude the rhetorical flourishes that raise voters' expectations yet don't commit parties unambiguously to certain actions or goals. Yet politicians seem disingenuous when they then resort to arguing about wording to explain away their apparent failings, and voters focused on the spirit of a promise are likely to smell a rat, even when the letter of a pledge has not been broken. Academics also give some credit to governments for partially fulfilling pledges, whereas most voters are probably less charitable.

And then there are the many promises made by politicians that are not included in manifestos, such as David Cameron's 2009 assurance that the National Health Service would suffer 'no more of those pointless reorganisations that aim for change but instead bring chaos'. Within three years, his government had legislated to do just that. (Ironically, it was the 2010 Conservative manifesto that reneged on Cameron's assurance, by committing the party to implement 'a reform plan to make the changes the NHS needs' – and so the government's Health and Social Care Bill was simultaneously both the keeping of a manifesto promise and the breaking of Cameron's earlier promise.) Although there is no systematic study of them, non-manifesto promises are probably more likely to be broken, not least because the process of drafting manifestos tends to subject parties' plans to better internal scrutiny. The symbolic status of manifesto pledges – which form the basis of a government's 'mandate' – also encourages politicians to take these promises more seriously. Yet, for most journalists and voters, a broken promise is a broken promise, whether or not it was in the manifesto.

While politicians don't always help themselves – they proclaim their own trustworthiness while denigrating their opponents' – the pervasive sense that parties break their election promises is also down to factors largely beyond their control. They have to contend with high levels of generalised public distrust (as discussed in Chapter 26), which predisposes voters to assume the worst about them, and negative media coverage, which serves to reinforce it. Stories celebrating the number of manifesto pledges fulfilled don't sell newspapers. Articles listing and denigrating a government's broken promises do.

For all these reasons, politicians have a reputation for reneging on their manifesto pledges. Given that this reputation is likely to persist, it is worth reflecting on some of the consequences for both the study and the practice of British democracy. For a start, voters' beliefs about political promises highlight a divide between political science and everyday views of politics. By focusing narrowly on the measurable, in this case specific pledges, academics sometimes overlook what matters most to voters. More importantly, the scepticism surrounding manifestos arguably weakens the foundations underpinning the mandate theory of democracy. It is harder for winning parties to claim legitimacy for their programmes after an election if most voters did not believe in the sincerity of their promises before it. As illustrated by the Ed Stone experience, politicians are now forced to go to ever greater lengths to convince voters of their sincerity. Such stunts may only serve to fuel voters' suspicions.

FURTHER READING

Useful studies of manifesto pledge fulfilment include Terry Royed's 'Testing the Mandate Model in Britain and the United States: Evidence from the Reagan and Thatcher Eras' (*British Journal of Political Science*, 1996) and Judith Bara's 'A Question of Trust: Implementing Party Manifestos' (*Parliamentary Affairs*, 2005). Citizens' attitudes towards politicians, including their concerns about political promise making, are covered by Nicholas Allen and Sarah Birch in *Ethics and Integrity in British Politics* (Cambridge University Press, 2015). Elin Naurin explores the 'pledge puzzle' using evidence from Sweden in *Election Promises, Party Behaviour and Voter Perceptions* (Palgrave Macmillan, 2011).

—CHAPTER 29—

Sex, lies and bribes: the judgement of public opinion

Richard Rose

When MPs behave badly they are representative of millions of voters who sometimes drink too much, engage in extramarital sex, or tell lies in their self-interest. Even though such behaviour is usually not a crime, it still violates standards of good behaviour endorsed by many people. Hence, British politicians who engage in bad behaviour would rather keep such behaviour private rather than be judged in the harsh court of public opinion.

International studies find Britain is relatively free from the worst kinds of public corruption – activities that in many countries enrich politicians through big-bucks bribes, kick-backs or dodgy contract allocation. However, that is not the only way in which public figures can violate public standards. The British media today is keener to run stories about MPs' behaviour that was kept out of the press in more deferential times.

The media judges the activities of politicians by whether they will make headline news. Names make news and by definition MPs are newsworthy. Yet, since many Britons are as distrustful of journalists as they are of politicians, people may discount 'shock' media disclosures as distorted or untrue.

The public is indeed discriminating in its assessment of how many politicians behave badly. The table below shows the results from a survey about how the public judges the behaviour of politicians in Britain, France and Spain. These countries differ in their ranking on the international Corruption Perception Index and, arguably, their standards for evaluating the behaviour of politicians.

While few see politicians as unblemished knights, less than a third of Britons think most or all MPs take money for favours or over-indulge in sex, drink or drugs. The French and Spaniards are only slightly more likely to think their MPs take money for favours and, perhaps due to a less aggressive media, are also slightly less likely to see their politicians over-indulging in hedonistic activities.

The form of bad behaviour the public perceive as most widespread is a violation of democratic values: politicians promising to do one thing if elected and then doing the opposite after winning. Almost three-quarters of Britons think that most politicians are hypocritical vote-seekers (even if the empirical evidence on this is much less clear cut, as discussed in the previous chapter); the proportion is higher still in France and in Spain. Moreover, a majority of every party's supporters take this view. In Britain 57 per cent of Conservative voters see politicians as hypocritical, as do seven out of eight UKIP supporters. In France, 72 per cent of Socialist Party voters see politicians as hypocrites and 92 per cent of supporters of the radical right National Front. In Spain, two-thirds of the supporters of the governing Popular Party see most politicians as hypocrites, along with nine-tenths of voters for the two new parties PODEMOS and Ciudadanos.

HOW MANY POLITICIANS BEHAVE BADLY? (% THINKING ALL, MOST)

	BRITAIN	FRANCE	SPAIN
Say one thing, do another	75	84	86
Take money for favours	31	35	38
Over-indulge sex, drink, drugs	30	26	19

Source: Nationwide sample surveys of 1,004 Britons, 1,003 French and 1,003 Spaniards, December 2015–January 2016, interviewed by telephone by Efficience3.

Bad behaviour is not criminal behaviour – as taking a bribe is – and the rules of the British Parliament are very narrow in assessing behaviour as deserving punishment. Less than 2 per cent of British MPs whose expenses were exposed were found guilty in a court of law, although scores were punished politically by not remaining in their seat in the next parliament, either being removed from office by the voters or more often encouraged into early retirement by their party leaders. The survey also offered the public a choice of alternative punishments for bad behaviour, ranging from apologising, to losing their job or going to jail. Offering an apology is often the preferred option for politicians who realise that denying published evidence would be inadequate. However, public opinion does not regard an apology as sufficient punishment for behaving in unacceptable ways.

A large majority of British respondents (69 per cent) think politicians should lose their job if they take money for doing a favour – though the British are actually more forgiving on this front than the Spanish or French, where around nine in ten would fire their politicians for this behaviour. A substantial minority of Britons (47 per cent) – probably seeing favours as a code word for bribery – favour a jail sentence for this behaviour. While only a small minority (12 per cent) think over-indulging in sex, drink or drugs deserves a jail sentence, a majority in Britain think that an MP should be punished by losing his or her job – something a majority of the French and Spanish also favour.

Theories of democracy postulate that voters dissatisfied with their elected representatives can punish hypocrites by voting for their opponent at the next general election. Three-fifths of British voters endorse this view and another quarter say they would not vote or were uncertain about what they would do if their MP ratted on election pledges. French views are similar. Spaniards are even readier to be punitive, with so large a proportion endorsing new parties at last December's election that it was impossible to form a government.

While over-indulgence and taking money for favours are individual forms of bad behaviour, telling voters one thing and doing another invites a collective judgement on political parties.

The perception of politicians as collectively hypocritical breeds collective distrust in MPs. Among Britons who think most politicians are hypocrites, 55 per cent distrust MPs compared to 20 per cent among those who see only a minority of their representatives as hypocritical. In France and Spain distrust is similarly high, but the net effect of hypocrisy is reduced because virtually everyone in those countries sees politicians as hypocrites. In short, the demand for politicians to clean up their act is not a reflection of British Victorian values but an expression of an apparently widespread 21st-century disillusionment with established political parties.

FURTHER READING

For further discussion, see *Survey of Public Attitudes towards Conduct in Public Life* (Committee on Standards in Public Life, 2013). Or Jennifer Jacquet's *Is Shame Necessary?* (Allen Lane, 2015) or *Using Open Data to Combat Corruption* by Richard Rose (University of Strathclyde Studies in Public Policy Number 518, 2015). The survey reported above was funded by a British ESRC grant to research The Experience of Corruption (ES/103482X/1).

CHAPTER 30

What do you do when the voters are wrong? Party funding reform

Sam Power

A poll carried out by the Electoral Reform Society (ERS) in 2014 found that 75 per cent of respondents believed that big donors had too much influence on British political parties, 65 per cent believed that donors could effectively buy knighthoods and other honours and 61 per cent believed the system for party funding was corrupt and needed to be changed. A Transparency International Global Corruption Barometer (GCB) poll taken a year before found a staggering 90 per cent of respondents thought the United Kingdom government was somewhat, to a large extent or entirely run by a few big entities acting in their own best interests – and 66 per cent felt that political parties were corrupt or extremely corrupt.

Taken at face value, the GCB poll meant that the UK would rank somewhere between Afghanistan (performs better) and Zimbabwe (performs worse) on the same measures. That is not a ranking that holds up to serious scrutiny. When the same poll asked about actual experiences of corruption, rather than perceptions of it, Britain came out much better.

However, a public belief that the political funding system is broken is widespread enough that politicians from all parties feel compelled to respond to it: in both 2010 and 2015 the Conservative, Labour and Liberal Democrat manifestos all included some form of pledge to introduce (or at least discuss) reform of party funding, and there have been two government-sponsored commissions on the subject in the last decade: the Hayden Phillips Review in 2006–07 and the Committee on Standards in Public Life (CSPL) Inquiry in 2010–11.

Yet while the public have a very negative view about existing party funding arrangements, they don't know much about how the party funding regime actually works. As the table shows, this disconnect is, in places, vast.

Indeed, despite much media coverage of large individual donations to political parties, respondents thought that business contributed more (and considerably more than they actually do) – although the knowledge that (often large) individual donations account for almost 50 per cent of parties' total income is, perhaps, unlikely to improve perceptions. The public also overestimate money from other sources, such as membership fees and state funding.

ESTIMATES OF SOURCES OF DONATIONS

SOURCE	ESTIMATED AVERAGE (%)	ACTUAL AVERAGE (%)	DIFFERENCE
Individuals	24	46	-22
Business/corporations	28	21	7
Trade unions	17	30	-13
Other	30	3	27

Source: Jennifer vanHeerde-Hudson and Justin Fisher, 'Parties Heed (with Caution): Public Knowledge of and Attitudes to Party Finance in Britain', *Party Politics*, 2013.

Attitudes about party funding seem to be fed by, and feed into, a wider mistrust of politicians and parties – with voters tending to run together funding and, for example, expenses – as in this response to a focus group conducted on behalf of the CSPL: 'They were saying about all these second homes and all these things they get expenses for … their second home with all this taxpayers money … TVs and whatever.'

This, in part, may explain why many voters reject the reform to party funding which is most popular with policy elites: a limit on annual donations made up by an increase in subsidies from the state, which was the solution endorsed by both Hayden Phillips and the CPSL as well as by many think tanks and reform groups. While the same ERS survey found 41 per cent of respondents felt that a publicly funded system would be fairer, 42 per cent favoured neither a public nor a privately funded system.

The oral evidence given to the CSPL inquiry is particularly informative because the public perception of corruption became a repeated bone of contention: the term 'perception' (or variants such as 'perceive'/'perceived') was mentioned 286 times. A belief frequently aired was that the perception of corruption itself demanded a response, even if it had little foundation in reality. This position is perhaps best summed up by Conservative MP for Croydon Central Gavin Barwell, who stated in his evidence: 'If you are saying: do I think it is unhealthy and that those large donors exert some effect on public policy, not in my direct experience. I certainly think that the public perception is that it is unhealthy and that, therefore, there may well be a case for doing something.'

With party funding, then, we find ourselves in a situation in which policy recommendations are being made (and put into manifestos) almost entirely on the basis of public perceptions. Yet we also know that this is a subject about which the public doesn't really know much at all – and where many of the experts on the subject think public perceptions of a problem are mistaken.

So what is to be done? There are good reasons to reform British party funding, but an uninformed perception of corruption, driven by a general distrust of politics and politicians, is probably not among them. For example, the sustainability of political parties' finances can be a real issue between general elections – it is much easier to solicit donations in general election years. Corruption might not be a major issue, but just funding basic political activities can be. The result is high-profile events like the Conservatives' Black-and-White Ball, in which wealthy donors bid for prizes such as going shoe shopping with Theresa May or running with Iain Duncan Smith – events which often reinforce negative public perceptions.

There is, therefore, an argument for gritting our teeth and making reform based on the current actual problems with the system – such as party sustainability. In countries across western Europe, this is what state subsidy provides – though the use of such subsidies rarely improves public corruption perceptions (and such systems come with their own problems, as discussed in Chapter 47). If party funding reform is framed as a silver bullet which will reduce anti-establishment feeling and end corruption, it is unlikely to succeed. Perhaps a more modestly framed reform proposal focused on helping parties fund the basic work of mobilising and talking to voters would succeed – or perhaps voters would angrily reject it as yet another establishment stitch-up. When it comes to the financing of politics there are no easy solutions.

FURTHER READING

The reports of the CSPL Inquiry, *Political Party Finance: Ending the Big Donor Culture* (2011), the Hayden Phillips Review, *Strengthening Democracy: Fair and Sustainable Funding of Political Parties* (2007), and the ERS's *Deal or No Deal: How to Put an End to Party Funding Scandals* can be found online. Also see the work of Justin Fisher on party finance, and in particular 'Parties Heed (with Caution): Public Knowledge of and Attitudes to Party Finance in Britain' (*Party Politics*, 2013), by Fisher and Jennifer vanHeerde-Hudson. For a wider perspective see *The Politics of Party Funding: State Funding to Political Parties and Party Competition in Western Europe* by Michael Koß (Oxford University Press, 2011).

'I'm never coming back to wherever this is.'

LABOUR MP PAT GLASS, WHILE CAMPAIGNING
IN SAWLEY, DERBYSHIRE IN 2016

CHAPTER 31

Two-party politics in a multi-party age: English local government

Colin Rallings

B ritain no longer has a two-party system. The old order has fragmented – shattered, even – and we are now in an era of multi-party politics. Everyone knows that.

But it seems no one told the English local councils. As David Cameron hailed the Conservatives' overall Commons majority as 'the sweetest victory of all' in May 2015, in local government a new script was being written.

Across the English shires and in the urban areas outside London, it was back to the 1960s. The Conservatives won six in ten of the more than 9,000 seats up for grabs. Labour did well too. In the metropolitan boroughs, including Birmingham, Manchester, Leeds and Newcastle, the party polled 45 per cent of the vote and won seven in ten of the contested seats.

Such was the scale of these victories that currently 83 per cent of English councils are now run by one of the two big parties, as the table shows. This is the highest proportion since the wholesale reorganisation of local government in the early 1970s. In the town halls of England two-party politics is back with a vengeance.

PARTY AFFILIATION OF COUNCILLORS AND PARTY CONTROL
OF COUNCILS, ENGLAND 1973–2015

PARTY AFFILIATION OF COUNCILLORS (%)				
	Conservative	Labour	Lib Dem	Other
1973	34	40	6	20
1999	30	41	21	8
2007	47	24	21	8
2015	48	33	9	9

PARTY CONTROL OF COUNCILS (%)					
	Conservative	Labour	Lib Dem	Independent	No overall control
1973	21	32	0	17	30
1999	19	37	7	3	34
2007	53	12	8	1	26
2015	55	28	2	1	14

To understand why this has happened when elsewhere the party system is fragmenting, two factors need to be taken into account. First, the changing patterns of party competition. Second, the behaviour of voters. The interaction between them explains the surprising survival of two-party local politics in a multi-party age.

Back in 1973, when the English local government system was radically restructured, local political competition was pretty tepid: on average two candidates contested each local vote. In about one in ten seats there was no election at all as councillors (many of them 'Independents') were returned unopposed. Things gradually heated up over the years. By 1999, when Liberal Democrats were pounding pavements and New Labour was in its pomp, each seat attracted 2.6 candidates and just 6 per cent of councillors did not face a contest in their ward.

The supply of candidates continues to grow. In 2015 an average of 3.4 candidates contested each seat. Only 200 seats – just 2.5 per cent – were unopposed. In urban areas, there were often more than four candidates per vacancy and it was rare to find any seat at all left uncontested.

Many of these candidates attract significant votes. Again, go back to 1973. Then, 10 per cent of all contested ward elections could be characterised as one-party contests, in which a single party so dominated the voting that none of its competitors came close to toppling it. About two-thirds were two-party competitive (most involving Labour–Conservative battles), leaving a quarter of contests to feature a three-or-more-way battle for votes.

Although two-party contests still dominated local elections by the close of the last century, the Liberal Democrats featured as one of the two parties in contention in half of such cases. The old order seemed under threat. At their peak in 2007, the Liberal Democrats were a competitive party in nearly six in ten of the local elections in England, and rivalry between any two of the now three major parties was commonplace in different areas. The Liberal Democrats not only beat Labour in the popular vote, they did so in seats won as well.

While things turned decidedly sour after this – Liberal Democrat councillors paying a heavy price for their party's membership of the coalition government – the impact on the competitiveness of local elections has been negligible, because as the Liberal Democrats faded, so UKIP rose. Indeed, the UKIP surge in 2013 and 2014 led to a further increase in three-party competition, with more than six in ten wards in 2015 warranting that description.

But neither UKIP nor the Greens, who have also enjoyed a small increase in votes, currently have a large enough core of support to equalise the ratio between votes polled and seats won. True, they field more candidates than before. True, they get more votes than before. But they hardly ever win.

The greater the number of parties and candidates at each contest, the lower the theoretical threshold for winning a seat. And that, ironically, suits the big boys best of all. It is usually a simple task for one or other of them to attract the core 35 per cent or so share of the vote needed to win. For the smaller parties such a level of support is often unattainable. Individual ward results then feed into even less representative council compositions. With fewer parties now on each council, it becomes easier for any one of them to chalk up the number of seats needed for an overall majority.

Consequently, the two main parties have been redrawing the local electoral map red and blue. Back in the 1990s, the Liberal Democrats liked to talk up the merits of 'balanced government' – what the rest of us call hung parliaments or councils. By 1999, a third of councils fell into the category of 'No Overall Control', run by minority administrations or coalitions of parties. The proportion is now less than half of that. And just six out of 351 local authorities in England still have a Liberal Democrat majority.

Unless and until another viable 'third' party emerges and acquires the skill of translating votes into seats, the new era of two-party-run local government in England is set to continue. Proponents of electoral reform bemoan what they see as the skewed and unresponsive nature of the present situation (the introduction of the Single Transferable Vote for Scottish local elections since 2007 has dramatically reduced the number of councils under single party control there) but the current government has no intention of changing a system which works so much to the advantage of its local representatives.

FURTHER READING

The data on which this chapter is based, and a wealth of other information about local electoral politics, can be accessed at www.electionscentre.co.uk. Commentaries by Colin Rallings and Michael Thrasher on each year's local elections have been published by *Local Government Chronicle* annually since 1984 and can also be found in the *Local Elections Handbook* series. The Electoral Reform Society regularly publishes pamphlets highlighting what it considers to be the unrepresentative nature of English local government, such as its *English Local Elections 2011* (ERS, 2011). David Denver has written on the impact of STV on Scottish local elections in 'A Quiet Revolution: STV and the Scottish Council Elections of 2007' (*Scottish Affairs*, 2007).

—CHAPTER 32—

Sophisticated voting systems for unsophisticated voters: grappling with the Supplementary Vote

Michael Thrasher

M any political scientists spend a lot of time thinking about voting
systems. From design to outcome there isn't much that does not
fascinate them about the process by which votes are cast and politicians are elected. But there is one feature of these systems and their
design that is often neglected: do voters really know what they are
doing when they vote?

Since 2000, a growing number of electors in Britain have been
invited to use the Supplementary Vote (SV) system. The Blair government chose this method for its new scheme of directly elected mayors
because, in its words, it is 'simple and easy to use'. The coalition government then also used SV as the system for electing the Police and
Crime Commissioners it introduced in 2012.

Despite the endorsement of Westminster politicians of various
partisan hues, it is not, in fact, a simple and easy-to-use system.

When an SV election is run alongside one that uses the traditional
'first past the post' system, the proportion of rejected ballots is much

higher for the SV election: about one in a hundred are rejected in a standard 'first past the post' race, but under SV the proportion is on average triple that. There were 50,000 invalid votes cast at the fifth London mayoral election in 2016, 2 per cent of the total. Admittedly, this is not a very high number, but it does reveal a degree of voter confusion sufficient to swing the result in close races.

Nor is that the only problem. There are features of SV that, unless people really engage with its complexities, are likely to lead to many votes effectively being excluded from the counting process.

From the voter's viewpoint, SV asks for a simple 'X' to be placed alongside the candidate of choice. But crucially, SV gives each voter two votes to cast, one in each of two adjacent columns placed alongside the list of candidates. Reading from left to right on the ballot paper, therefore, the voter sees the name of each candidate, then party description and logo, next a first box requiring a 'X' and then another box for a second cross.

Any candidate winning more than half of the first votes is automatically elected. If no outright winner emerges, the top two candidates following the first count remain in the contest but all other candidates are then eliminated with any second votes on these ballots cast in favour of those remaining being transferred. It is the combination of first and second votes that determines the winner.

For a small minority of voters this feature of SV is great: it allows them the freedom to cast a first vote for their preferred candidate but then to plump for one of the two front runners likely to battle it out in the second round.

But what about most other voters?

For some there is a temptation to skip the instructions printed on the ballot paper and simply plonk a single cross in the second, right-most column, which is how people vote in a general election. Under SV, this is an invalid vote and won't count, since the box for the first vote is left empty.

Other participants will vote for the same candidate twice, although it is unclear whether that behaviour is the act of the strong partisan (I always vote for this party and no other) or simply a person that doesn't understand the system. Whichever is the case, these second votes cannot count towards determining the winner. If they are cast for one of the two front runners then they cannot be transferred during the second count. Two votes cast for candidates destined for elimination are also ineligible for subsequent transfer.

The volume of such votes prompted the Electoral Commission to produce a leaflet to assist voters with SV. This helpfully stated that a vote for the first choice candidate should go in the first column, a vote in the second column for second choice candidates and that 'your first and second choices should be different'. To little avail, it seems.

In the first SV election, that for the London mayor in 2000, about 85 per cent of the second votes that were cast did not feature in the eventual election of Ken Livingstone. Perhaps this was because SV was a novel system.

But even by the fourth London mayoral election held in 2012, voters did not seem to have come to terms with the intricacies of SV. The mayoral campaign was dominated by the incumbent Boris Johnson and the former mayor, Ken Livingstone. They were the clear front runners. Yet, 1.4 million second votes were cast by people who voted for either Johnson or Livingstone in the first round. These votes are irrelevant, yet they amount to 80 per cent of all the second votes cast.

The majority of people who used the second vote still do not seem to realise that casting a second vote in this way has no impact on the outcome. In the most recent London mayoral contest, eight in ten voters cast a first vote for either Sadiq Khan or Zac Goldsmith. That still left half a million second votes available for transfer from ballots supporting candidates eliminated after the first round. In fact, only 46 per cent of these second votes were eventually transferred.

Instead, the Green candidate, a very distant third after the first count and eliminated alongside ten other candidates, saw almost half a million second votes cast in her favour. Over a million second votes were cast in favour of candidates that lost their election deposits by polling under 5 per cent of the total first votes.

Logically speaking, if a voter supports one of the two clear front runners in an SV election there is no point in casting another vote. Similarly, if a voter is determined to support only one party there really is no point in casting a second vote. Those points did seem to be getting through. The proportion of London voters not using their second vote at all began to rise, albeit slowly. At the 2004 election it stood at 15 per cent, rising to 17 per cent in 2008 and 20 per cent in 2012. In 2016, however, it fell back to 15 per cent, suggesting that for most of London's voters, the rules of an SV election remain opaque.

FURTHER READING

For a detailed critique of Supplementary Vote see Henk Van der Kolk et al.'s 'Electing Mayors: A Comparison of Different Electoral Procedures' (*Local Government Studies*, 2004). An examination written by the same authors of its early application for the London mayoral vote can be found in 'The Effective Use of the Supplementary Vote in Mayoral Elections: London 2000 and 2004' (*Representation*, 2006). For a more positive view of SV's merits see Patrick Dunleavy's various blog posts, including 'Electing the London Mayor and Police Commissioners in England and Wales: How to Use Your Two Votes Well' (2016).

— CHAPTER 33—

The freedom to make identical decisions: the devolution paradox

Ailsa Henderson

Public opinion surveys consistently show that Scots want their Parliament to have more influence over their lives. But polls also show that many Scots want policy uniformity across the whole of the UK. In other words, they want the Scottish Parliament to make more of the decisions affecting their lives, but they want the outcomes of those decisions to be identical to outcomes in the rest of the UK.

It's not just Scots either. One study asked people in France, Germany, Austria, Spain and the UK if they want the regional level to be more important – regional meaning large sub-state regions like Scotland or Catalonia – and they often said yes. But when asked whether they wanted the region to control additional areas of policy like health or taxes, education or the environment, a sizeable portion (between 20 and 40 per cent) of voters said no. So voters want their region to be more powerful than it is at the moment, but they don't necessarily want it to control big policy areas. Those living in regions with stronger historical identities like Catalonia, Wales or Scotland were less likely to produce this sort of policy paradox (with roughly 10 per cent or so holding such views), but even in these cases the devolution paradox was still clear.

Furthermore, if we ask people whether they want policy decisions to vary across regions, the answer is also often no, regardless of whether they want the region to exert more influence. The notion that someone living in another part of the state should have access to medicine otherwise unavailable elsewhere, or should pay less for university, or should be sentenced more strictly for committing the same crime as someone else, is very unappealing to voters, despite the fact that this is an obvious consequence of giving regions more power, as they say they want. This type of uniformity paradox is even more prevalent. In 2011, support for policy uniformity ranged from roughly 20 per cent in Scotland and Catalonia to over 60 per cent in some Austrian länder. The constitutional architecture of the state seems to matter little; indeed those living in federal states where regions have more powers often had more paradoxical attitudes.

This paradox remains alive and well in both Scotland and Wales. Scots want the Scottish Parliament to be more powerful, and yet – as the table below shows – many are also steadfastly opposed to policy variation across the UK.

SUPPORT FOR POLICY UNIFORMITY

	SCOTLAND	ENGLAND	WALES
Unemployment benefit	51	65	59
University tuition fees	34	63	45
Paying for elderly care	47	67	56
Punishment of young offenders	58	76	68
Prescription charges	37	72	41
Income tax	49	68	61

Source: Smith Survey 2014. Results are column percentages. For example 51 per cent of Scots think unemployment benefits should be uniform across the UK.

Even in cases where the figures drop below 50 per cent, uniform policy is still the most popular option among those who expressed a preference. English support for policy uniformity is greatest but while the results are more mixed for Scotland and Wales we see considerable support for policy uniformity even on issues where there is current variation, such as punishment of young offenders.

Why? First, public knowledge about which level of government is responsible for policy is generally low – this is as true in more established federal countries as it is in the relatively young devolved settlements in the UK. Many Scottish voters still think that most policy areas are governed by Westminster, so their call for more powers can come from a mistaken belief that London controls more than it does.

Second, attitudes to policy variation appear to be influenced by a fear of losing out. Individuals don't mind policy variation if they are on the receiving end of more generous provision or a better outcome, but become very unhappy with policy variation if it means getting the short straw. This might explain why Scots don't object so much to variation in prescription charges, tuition fees and care for the elderly, since these are more generous in Scotland. If asked whether varying levels of tax was problematic because a) it would lead to tax competition, b) it would lead someone to lose out (pay higher tax) or c) it would lead someone to enjoy greater benefits (pay lower tax), the most popular objection in Scotland, Wales and England was the idea that someone would lose out.

However, not everyone gets caught up in this paradoxical thinking. Some are more likely to have paradoxical views than others, and while in the aggregate we see a lot of variation, at the individual level people tend to be more consistent. In comparative studies, those with a greater sense of national identity and who think the region should have more influence typically want it to have more policy control and also want (or at least accept) more policy variation between regions. Those who believe the region is wealthier are also more likely to support policy control and policy variation (reasoning, logically, that if conditions are allowed to vary between regions their region stands to gain). Conversely, those living in poorer regions are less keen on both regional policy control and variation. This fits with the polling data highlighting a widespread fear of losing out.

Returning to Scotland, we know that among those who expressed a preference a majority want policy uniformity. What about those who want variation? Here we find that individuals who support policy variation want Scotland to have *both* higher benefits and lower taxes than in the rest of the UK. But that's another paradox for another day.

FURTHER READING

For a collection of essays on how this operates in different contexts, see Scott Greer's edited volume *Devolution and Social Citizenship in the UK* (Policy Press, 2009), especially the chapters by Keith Banting, Charlie Jeffery and Daniel Wincott. The original article using comparative data is Ailsa Henderson et al.'s 'Reflections on the Devolution Paradox: A Comparative Examination of Multilevel Citizenship' (*Regional Studies*, 2013). Greater detail for specific countries may be found in *Citizenship after the Nation State* (Palgrave Macmillan, 2014). For an analysis of recent data relating to Scotland and England, see Ailsa Henderson et al.'s 'National Identity or National Interest: Scottish, English and Welsh Attitudes to the Constitutional Debate' (*Political Quarterly*, 2015).

—CHAPTER 34—

It wasn't 'The Vow' wot won it: the Scottish independence referendum

Rob Johns

The sequence of events seems clear enough. After months of trailing badly in the polls, the Yes side in the 2014 Scottish independence referendum rapidly narrowed the gap to the point at which a couple of polls actually showed a narrow majority for independence. Panicked, the Better Together campaign – in a move spearheaded by Gordon Brown – came up with 'The Vow'. On the front page of the *Daily Record* on Tuesday 16 September, two days before polling, the three main Westminster leaders made a very public pledge of 'extensive new powers' for the Scottish Parliament. This last-ditch promise of further devolution effectively removed the status quo from the ballot paper and replaced it with a 'more powers for Scotland' option that had been the most popular all along. And the poll drift towards Yes was reversed, culminating in the eventually clear 55–45 victory for No. Case closed? Not so fast.

A first simple question to ask is about timing. The Vow cannot have caused a shift in the polls that was already visible before its publication. And as the figure below shows, there was already just such a change in the polls *before* the Vow was published. In this 'poll of polls' graph, where each point represents the average of the past four polls (to smooth out the wrinkles caused by the ±3% margin of error in any individual poll), the turning-point is in polls completed by 12 September, four days *before* that famous *Daily Record* cover.

But perhaps the Vow was only the ceremonial sign-off of more powers – powers that had already been heralded in a speech by Gordon Brown on 8 September? Maybe it was that promise of enhanced devolution that halted Yes's progress? The problem with this argument is that, as also shown in the figure, backing for independence continued to climb *after* Brown's speech. Neither of the interventions highlighted in the graph seems to have triggered a downturn in Yes support.

POLL-OF-POLLS TREND, SCOTLAND, 15 AUGUST–17 SEPTEMBER 2014

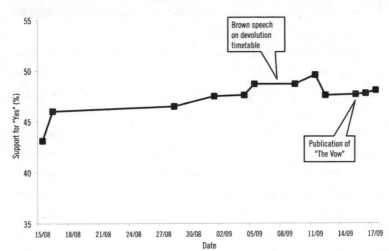

One possible reason for this is that the Vow was not widely believed. The Scottish Referendum Study asked respondents how likely they thought it was that, in the event of a No vote, 'Westminster would transfer substantially more powers to the Scottish Parliament'. If we break the final month of campaigning into four weeks, we find that this outcome was thought 'very' or 'fairly' likely by 36 per cent of people in week 1, and by 40 per cent in week 4. The pledge of further devolution, and more generally the furious cross-party campaigning that culminated in the Vow, seems to have done little to dent widespread and entrenched scepticism. Look only at the small minority of undecided voters in this survey, and you see still more scepticism. In week 4, only 27 per cent of them thought that further devolution was likely in the event of a No – barely different from the 26 per cent in week 1. No sign here of waverers being won over to No by the promise of more powers.

Another way to approach this is to consider the counterfactual: that is, what would have happened had the Vow not been made? Might the Yes momentum have been halted anyway? If we had no other explanation for that polling reversal, it would be harder to deny the Vow some credit.

But in fact there *is* a compelling alternative explanation. The norm in constitutional referendums is for exactly the late swing to the status quo that we saw in the days before 18 September, and the bigger the proposed change, the likelier (and larger) that late swing tends to be. It doesn't always happen, of course – as we discovered from the 'Brexit' vote in June 2016 – but it usually does when, as in the Scottish independence referendum, both sides agree that a big change is in prospect. Certainly the Better Together campaigners (who coined their own nickname of 'Project Fear') sought to present an independence vote as a leap off a precipice, from which it warned Scots to draw back. These are precisely the conditions in which voters who have flirted with change often decide against it in the final analysis. The likelihood of such a late swing was one reason why No remained the clear favourite with the bookmakers even as the polls narrowed.

Rather than the Vow causing the No victory, then, the two instead share a common cause. That common cause is those polls – one published on 7 September, the next a week later – that showed a Yes lead. These not only triggered the panic in the Better Together campaign that produced the Vow, but also brought home to Scottish voters that independence was a real possibility. And when presented with that real possibility, some were not ready to take the plunge. Alex Salmond himself would later say that the first Yes lead came a week too early for his campaign.

So why have so many people since concluded that the Vow was the clincher? One explanation is a coincidence of timing. Until the chronology is scrutinised in detail, it can easily seem that the Vow triggered the late swing back to No. Another is straightforwardly political. It was in the interests of those who supported independence to argue that the Vow had been decisive and that Scotland would have voted Yes but for what they claimed was a confidence trick, rather than to focus on their failure to convince enough voters of the case – especially the economic case – for independence. Then there are some persistent biases in human reasoning: we are prone to see causality where there is mere coincidence or correlation; we are prone to simplify; and we favour explanations based on agency – that is, the actions taken by leading figures in the drama – rather than structural factors like the risk-aversion highlighted above.

Indeed, if we must reduce the referendum to one simple causal explanation, then 'It's the economy, stupid' is probably a more convincing one. This does not mean that the Vow was entirely irrelevant. Increasing confidence about further devolution may have been another reason – alongside last-minute caution plus a stronger turnout among No supporters – why the winning margin was wider than the final polls suggested. Nevertheless, the outcome in 2014 was predictable (and predicted) in advance without the Vow, and it can be explained in retrospect without it too.

FURTHER READING

For a vivid account of this particular referendum campaign, read Joe Pike's *Project Fear: How an Unlikely Alliance Left a Kingdom United but a Country Divided* (Biteback, 2014). On late swing in referendums in general, see Alan Renwick's 'Don't Trust Your Poll Lead: How Public Opinion Changes during Referendum Campaigns' in *Sex, Lies and the Ballot Box* (Biteback, 2014). Finally, Richard Nadeau et al. highlight the role of risk-aversion in referendum voting in 'Attitude Towards Risk-Taking and Individual Choice in the Quebec Referendum on Sovereignty' (*British Journal of Political Science*, 1999).

—CHAPTER 35—

It's not Scotland: Wales's enduring electoral semi-distinctiveness

Roger Scully

One of the most striking statistics to emerge from the 2015 UK general election was that while in Scotland UKIP stood candidates in forty-one of fifty-nine seats and every one failed to get the 5 per cent vote share needed to retain their £500 electoral deposit, in Wales UKIP stood candidates in all forty seats and every one retained their deposit. But the differences pertained to much more than just UKIP. Labour were crushed in Scotland, yet retained their leading position in Wales. Though a disappointment for Labour, who made a small net loss in seats when they had expected to advance, 2015 was still the twentieth successive general election (in a run stretching from 1935) where Labour won the most votes *and* a majority of seats in Wales.

Alongside continuing Labour success in Wales came the persistent weakness of Plaid Cymru. Unlike their sister party in Scotland, the SNP, Plaid made little progress in 2015. This reflects not only differences between the two parties but also broader contrasts in the two nations' political landscape. Wales has had no independence referendum, nor the broader surge in political engagement that came with it in Scotland. For whatever reason – stronger social links with England, an awareness of Wales' relative economic weakness and dependence on UK subsidies, or simply the fact that no significant political force spends much time advocating the idea – support for independence in Wales remains low: at or below 10 per cent in most polls.

Sure, the Welsh people have come to support significant autonomy within the UK. After rejecting the idea overwhelmingly in a 1979 referendum, and then only endorsing it very narrowly in a second vote in 1997, people in Wales rapidly came to accept devolution. For more than a decade devolution has been the clear 'settled will' of a substantial majority of people in Wales, with some public desire to extend it into currently undevolved policy areas, such as policing. But there is little desire for an independent Welsh state. Wales is not Scotland.

But Wales is not England, either.

The advances of the Conservatives and UKIP in 2015 did make Wales look superficially rather similar to England. Writing in the *London Review of Books*, Ross McKibbon suggested that 'The Tories did well in Wales ... part of a process by which Wales is becoming assimilated into English politics'. Put bluntly, this interpretation doesn't stand much scrutiny.

The figure shows scores for Scotland and Wales in all general elections from 1945 on an Index of Dissimilarity, a measure of how much the electoral fortunes of parties in Scotland and Wales have differed from those in England; it runs from a possible 0 (where all parties gained exactly the same vote share as they did in England at that year's election) to 100 (where all the votes were gained by parties that won no votes at all in England). As can be seen, for the first half of the post-war era, Scotland was more similar to England in its voting behaviour than Wales was. There was a sudden upwards move in the index in Scotland in 1974 – the year when the SNP first became a serious electoral threat to the main UK-wide parties – and Scotland has been more electorally distinct from England than Wales has at every subsequent general election. But the extent of those differences with England increased markedly in 2010, and dramatically further with the SNP surge in 2015.

The picture for Wales is very different – a more consistent pattern, with only modest fluctuations in the level of Welsh electoral distinctiveness. The index reaches its highest points in 1987 and 1992 – when Labour (led by the Welshman Neil Kinnock) unsurprisingly did particularly well in Wales. But Welsh electoral distinctiveness edged only marginally downwards in 2015, and towards the long-term average. Wales remained roughly as electorally distinct from England in 2015 as it has been since 1945.

INDEX OF DISSIMILARITY, SCOTLAND AND WALES (COMPARED TO ENGLAND), 1945–2015 GENERAL ELECTIONS

These findings reflect a broader, defining reality of Welsh political life – the ambiguity of Wales's national status. Wales has long had its own language and culture, and a deeply rooted sense of national distinctiveness. And after several hundred years when it was, for the purposes of government, dealt with as little more than a part of England, Wales's national status has developed a governmental dimension. Wales today is a self-conscious and at least partially self-governing nation.

Yet one can, equally correctly, point out that alongside a strong and persisting sense of Welsh national identity, the majority of people in Wales also affirm an identity with Britain. They feel, to some extent, both Welsh and British. It is also true to say that Wales's political autonomy under devolution remains distinctly limited: in various respects, Wales is less self-governing than Scotland or Northern Ireland, or indeed many other sub-state nations and regions. And it is further true that the news-media most people in Wales consume, through which they receive much of their information about politics, government and current affairs, are overwhelmingly London-based and London-focused.

In short, Wales is both a partially self-governing nation yet also part of a London-centric, British political space. This gives politics in Wales what Balsom and colleagues aptly described in 1983 as 'a bifocal perspective', Welsh as well as British. Such bifocalism permeates all aspects of political life in Wales, including elections.

FURTHER READING

For McKibbon's discussion of the electoral distinctiveness – or not – of Wales, see 'Labour dies again' (*London Review of Books*, 4 June 2015). For Balsom et al.'s discussion of Welsh electoral 'bifocalism' see 'The Red and the Green: Patterns of Partisan Choice in Wales' (*British Journal of Political Science*, 1983). For a much broader discussion of both historical and contemporary electoral politics in Wales, see Roger Scully's *Elections in Wales* (University of Wales Press, 2017).

'The plural of anecdote is data.'

RAYMOND WOLFINGER (ALMOST ALWAYS NOW RECOUNTED AS
'DATA IS NOT THE PLURAL OF ANECDOTE', THUS COMPLETELY
MISSING THE POINT WOLFINGER WAS TRYING TO MAKE)

—CHAPTER 36—

From eccentric to social mainstream? The revival of party membership

Lynn Bennie

A distant observer of UK politics might get the impression that joining a political party has suddenly become fashionable. Since 2013,
membership of Britain's political parties has grown, spectacularly in
some cases. Labour membership nearly doubled in 2015, sparked by
the party's leadership election. The English and Welsh Greens experienced substantial injections of new members from 2014, overtaking
UKIP, whose membership base had itself doubled from 2012. The
Liberal Democrats, bruised by coalition, managed to recover some
strength in 2015, taking them close to the size of membership they
had before entering government. Even Conservative membership
grew a little, despite a long stint in government.

Events in Scotland were even more remarkable. Following the 2014
referendum on Scottish independence, the Scottish National Party
(SNP) and Scottish Green Party (SGP) (both pro-independence)
experienced an astonishing influx of members. Over ten years, SNP
and SGP membership multiplied by a factor of nine, with most of the

growth occurring in the aftermath of the referendum. At the time of the referendum vote, the SNP had a membership of around 26,000; within nine months it had risen to 115,000. In the same period, Scottish Green members increased from 1,500 to 9,000.

Party membership has been in decline for so long that speculation about the death of parties had become part of contemporary political wisdom. Decline has occurred in other established democracies, usually explained by changes in societies that reduce the 'supply' of members – such as a greater range of leisure opportunities or the expansion in alternative ways of engaging in politics – but membership loss has been especially severe in Britain, making the recent growth in recruitment all the more curious. And it conflicts with our understanding of citizen engagement. Modern electorates are, we are always being told, increasingly 'critical' of politics, hostile to traditional parties and traditional methods of political participation. So a sudden surge in party membership was, to say the least, unexpected.

BRITISH PARTY MEMBERSHIP 2006–2015

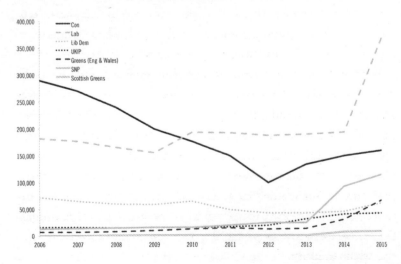

The member surges have some stand-out characteristics. For a start, their sheer scale is striking. The last time Labour had as many members as in 2015 was in 1998, at the height of the New Labour honeymoon. The scale of the SNP intake means it can claim to be the first mass party in a generation – one in every thirty-seven Scots adults now belong to it. (In the UK as a whole, around one in a hundred adults are members of a party.) Secondly, the surges have been swift. At the peak of the SNP surge, thousands of new recruits were joining each day. Thirdly, the biggest boosts to membership appear to be responses to electoral *failure*. Parties who lost an election (Labour and the Lib Dems in 2015) or a referendum (the SNP in 2014) have gained far more supporters than those who won at the ballot box. In the past, we assumed that party success attracted members.

Lastly, the surges have some qualities we associate more with social movements than political parties. These typically involve grassroots networks of volunteer activists, advocating change at the level of civil society, not via centralised elites. Momentum, the Corbyn-supporting campaign network, is often viewed in this way. The Yes campaign for Scottish independence also had a clear grassroots dynamic, where traditional political meetings and rallies coexisted with modern online activities, creating networks of potential party members.

For those who study party membership, such developments are difficult to explain. An upbeat interpretation is that more people are inspired by party politics than in a long time. Both the Scottish independence campaign and Corbynmania involved a sense of hope and optimism for those they attracted. A positive vision can be inspiring and encourage political engagement. Could this be a renaissance of political activism, when it becomes socially acceptable, even trendy, to join a party? Given the widespread lack of respect for parties among the electorate, and that party members remain a minority group, this seems unlikely.

A more pessimistic view is that we are observing a new form of protest politics, born of disillusionment with the political establishment; that is, a more negative dynamic may be driving events, amounting to 'one in the eye' for the established order. This would explain why losing parties are gaining members most quickly, and the rhetoric of the SNP, Greens and Jeremy Corbyn all involve a large element of hostility to mainstream 'politics as usual'. Increases in membership may even be interpreted as a sign of weakness. If they are not careful, by becoming social movements parties can appear to abandon the pursuit of power. This is plausible in the case of Labour, though not the SNP, a governing party which has been strengthened by the membership surge.

Perhaps the individual parties' stories are too different for a general explanation. The genuinely exceptional increases have occurred in Scotland, where grassroots activity in reaction to an unusually powerful political campaign over independence triggered a wave of political party membership. In the Labour Party, new (and possibly returning) members joined to take part in an unusual leadership contest where, for the first time in decades, a radical left candidate stood a chance of winning. The Lib Dems received a boost to their activist base when the party was liberated from government.

What are the consequences of these events? In the past, parties struggled to attract young people and women (again, an international phenomenon, but pronounced in the UK). Party members appeared weird in that so few people joined parties at all and those that did were disproportionately old and male. We don't yet know if the new influx is any different.

Most academics in this field have argued for decades that attracting members brings valuable resources to parties, boosting their organisational and financial strength. Injections of new members can be transformative for parties like the Greens, who struggle to compete with bigger, wealthier competitors.

But new waves of members can create tensions in parties. In Labour there has been speculation about a kind of insurgency, creating division and radically altering the character of the party. This assumes that the new recruits have different motivations and expectations of membership, perhaps with more pronounced anti-system attitudes. In truth, we don't yet know whether motivations to join are changing – or if new members are bound to be disappointed.

FURTHER READING

Patrick Seyd and Paul Whiteley pioneered the modern study of party members in *Labour's Grass Roots* (Clarendon Press, 1992). For cross-national comparison see 'Going, Going… Gone? The Decline of Party Membership in Contemporary Europe' by Ingrid van Biezen et al. (*European Journal of Political Research*, 2012) or Emilie van Haute and Anika Gauja's *Party Members and Activists* (Routledge, 2015). In *Ruling the Void* (Verso, 2013) Peter Mair associates 'seemingly unstoppable' membership decline with a 'hollowing out' of modern democracies. Susan Scarrow's *Beyond Party Members* (Oxford University Press, 2015) highlights parties' adaptation to declining memberships. James Mitchell et al.'s *The Scottish National Party: Transition to Power* (Oxford University Press, 2012) is a study of the SNP and its membership in the late 2000s.

CHAPTER 37

Members are not the only fruit: the role of party supporters

Justin Fisher

For years, the received wisdom was that political parties were in some kind of crisis on account of falling membership. This is no longer quite so true in Britain (as discussed in the previous chapter) but while the downward trend has now at least temporarily reversed, concerns remain about the democratic and electoral consequences of the previous long decline, which continues in other countries. In democratic terms, the fear is that, as membership declines, so party elites will increasingly dominate, especially in countries with extensive state funding, which some argue shields parties from the need to engage with their supporters to raise money. And in electoral terms, the concern is that party members are an essential part of political campaigning, yielding electoral pay-offs and increased electoral participation. With fewer members, who will do the door knocking and leaflet delivering?

Parties have responded to these pressures in different ways. One has been to throw open involvement in party decision making to a wider group than just their members. In Australia, Italy, Germany, Scandinavia, Spain, Taiwan and Mexico, party supporters (who are not formal members) have become more involved in party decisions. In France in 2011, the Socialist Party used a primary system to select its presidential candidate, opening voting to any French adult who signed a pledge that they supported the 'values of the left' and paid a fee of €1.

Since 2005 the British Conservatives have experimented with primaries for a handful of candidate selections. But the most striking British example was the 2015 election for the leadership of the Labour Party, which was open not only to members, but also to any 'registered supporter' who paid £3 and declared they shared the values and aims of the party. Not only did Labour's formal membership rise significantly after the 2015 general election, but more than 100,000 registered supporters voted in the leadership election, some 25 per cent of all the votes cast. Add in affiliated supporters, those members of affiliated organisations such as trade unions who are not full individual members, and the figure rises to more than 170,000 – 42 per cent of those voting. One interesting consequence here was the attention given to allegations of 'entryism', both by left-wing supporters of the victor, Jeremy Corbyn, and by political opponents of Labour, keen to see the apparently 'unelectable' Corbyn become leader, with Corbyn attracting 84 per cent of the newly registered supporters' votes. In the end, Corbyn also won comfortably among formal members (securing 50 per cent of their votes), but it may be that his surprise election will make other parties' elites more cautious in the future about opening up such important elections to those outside the formal membership.

In terms of election campaigning, parties have for some years been adapting to declines in membership – not least by using technology to take on important tasks that previously party members would have undertaken, such as addressing envelopes and reminding people to vote on polling day. Developments such as direct mail, telephone voter identification and e-campaigning have also meant that more voters can be contacted and in more personalised ways. But parties have also begun to use non-member supporters to help them out in election campaigns.

In 2010, for example, for the three principal parties in Britain (the Conservatives, Labour and the Liberal Democrats), 78 per cent of local parties had help from supporters – people who sympathised with a party but were not paid-up members – in key election campaign tasks. These supporters formed a significant proportion of each local party's volunteer force – a mean of eighteen supporters per constituency. In 2015, the figures for both Conservative and Labour campaigns were similar: around 70 per cent of local parties recruited supporters to help them out. Such supporters are not quite as active as full members – they do about two-thirds of the things that members do – and tend to be less likely to engage in face-to-face contact with voters, something that voters value and which generally produces the most significant electoral pay-offs. However, important work like leafleting, taking numbers at polling stations and helping out at the campaign office is almost as likely to be undertaken by supporters as it is by members.

Moreover, supporters do not simply increase the level of activity where members are already active. In the case of both the Conservatives and Labour, the existing strength of the local party organisation has little impact on the level of supporters' activity. Supporters not only complement existing activity, they also supplement it, adding something extra, which enhances these activities, especially where the existing party structure is less strong, and make positive independent contributions to the intensity of campaign efforts overall. Parties could not do without members, but where member activity continues to decline, neither, it seems, can they do without the less firmly attached, but still active and valuable, supporters.

But one of the problems with a growing reliance on semi-attached supporters becomes clear when we look at the Liberal Democrats. In 2010, some 86 per cent of Liberal Democrat campaigns featured supporters as part of their volunteer team. In 2015, the comparable figure was 45 per cent. Supporters may be fair-weather friends, less loyal than formal members, and they may vanish when the going gets tough. Were these observations to be repeated over time, such a shift could make electoral competition more volatile. In other words, an increasing reliance on supporters, who may be less loyal than formal members, would accelerate the decline of parties experiencing a dip in popularity. All of this is to say that parties are evolving rather than necessarily declining, and that membership is clearly not the only source of grass roots involvement – it's not all doom and gloom. But equally, the example of the Liberal Democrats in 2015 suggests that while members may not be the only fruit, they are more nourishing for parties in barren times.

FURTHER READING

For supporter involvement in political parties in Britain see 'Members Are Not the Only Fruit: Volunteer Activity in British Political Parties at the 2010 General Election' by Justin Fisher et al. (*British Journal of Politics and International Relations*, 2014). In the past few years, there has been a flurry of comparative publications, including: Hilmar L. Mjelde's 'Non-Member Participation in Political Parties: A Framework for Analysis and Selected Examples from Scandinavia' (*Representation*, 2015); Anika Guaja's 'The Individualisation of Party Politics: The Impact of Changing Internal Decision-Making on Policy Development and Citizen Engagement' (*British Journal of Politics and International Relations*, 2015); and Giulia Sandri and Antonella Seddone's 'Sense or Sensibility? Political Attitudes and Voting Behaviour of Party Members, Voters, and Supporters of the Italian Centre-Left' (*Italian Political Science Review*, 2015).

—CHAPTER 38—

Tuned in to public life but turned off politics? Voluntary organisations and political participation

Christopher Prosser

We are living in a golden age of public participation in Britain. Levels of charitable giving, volunteering and membership of voluntary organisations are at record highs. British people have never been as charitable or involved with civil society as they are right now.

At the same time, political participation has never been lower. Measured as a proportion of the voting-age population, turnout at general elections has hovered around 60 per cent for the last four elections. And, although political parties have gained members recently (see Chapter 36), this follows many decades of steady decline. Even with the recent upturn, the number of party members is still only around a tenth of the level in the 1950s, the high-water mark of party membership in Britain.

What explains the divergence between these different forms of civic participation?

One answer is that people have been turned off by the spin, sleaze and cynicism of modern politics and have turned to alternative forms of participation instead. From this standpoint, the key to demo-cratic renewal is to make politics more like other forms of modern participation.

A more pessimistic view is that modern forms of engagement are not 'real' participation at all. In this view, 'clicktivism' and 'cheque-book activism' are quick and easy forms of participation that do not lead to further engagement – we sign a cheque or click a button, but take things no further. From this perspective the apparent rise in civic engagement is simply an artefact of the fact that some forms of participation have become a lot easier, even as 'real' participation (which remains as hard as ever) has actually declined.

Unfortunately for both of these arguments, one fact suggests they are both wrong: people who participate in non-political civil society are also much *more* likely to participate in more traditional forms of politics than those that do not. Although some of the newer kinds of online engagement do not seem to encourage participation on their own (as discussed in Chapter 13), this is not true of more established civil society organisations. People who engage with civic organisa-tions like the National Trust or the Women's Institute are also more likely to engage with party politics.

That this is the case is easy to show using data on political partici-pation from the 2015 British Election Study combined with data on membership of six different voluntary organisations and a variable for membership of any trade union collected by YouGov for the same respondents. The graph below shows the proportion of members and non-members of each of these organisations who report having voted in the 2015 general election.

The National Trust is one of the largest membership organisations in Britain, with 4.25 million members in 2015 and a further 300,000 members of the National Trust for Scotland. Seventy-nine per cent of members of the National Trust report having voted in 2015 compared to 58 per cent of non-members. In other words, just under one million more National Trust members turned out to vote in 2015 compared to the same size group of non-members.

Although they differ considerably in their aims, and the demographics and political views of their membership, there is a consistent pattern across the different organisations shown here: in each case members are much more likely to report having voted than non-members. The size of the differences ranges from Greenpeace, whose members are fourteen percentage points more likely to say they voted than non-members, to the Scouts, whose adult volunteers were twenty-two percentage points more likely to have voted than non-Scouts.

REPORTED TURNOUT AMONG MEMBERS AND NON-MEMBERS OF SEVEN MEMBERSHIP ORGANISATIONS

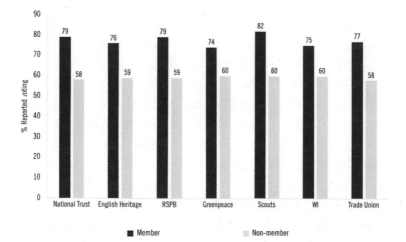

Source: British Election Study, 2015

People who are members of one or more of these organisations are also more likely to contact MPs or local councillors, sign petitions, take part in public demonstrations, and join or volunteer to do work for political parties.

What accounts for these differences in participation? A large part of it is down to differences in the sorts of people who like to participate in organisations – they are also often the kinds of people (older, better off, middle-class) who are more likely to take part in elections anyway. But even after accounting for a range of factors like age, income, social class, education, personality and interest in politics, members of voluntary organisations are still more likely to turn out to vote than non-members. Taking part in voluntary associations really matters politically.

The political scientist Robert Putnam has argued that voluntary associations encourage habits of cooperation and participation, and strengthen the social bonds between members. Research into turnout has consistently shown that social influences are the key to understanding why some people vote and others do not. If you believe that other people would think the worse of you for not voting, you are more likely to actually turn out to vote yourself. Voluntary associations both encourage the norm of participation and create ties that reinforce that norm.

Why then is political participation declining while these other forms of participation, which encourage it, are increasing? The reason for the apparent disconnect is perfectly illustrated by the different fortunes of the National Trust and trade unions, which in many ways are demographic opposites – someone with a professional occupation is about twice as likely to be a National Trust member as they are to be a trade union member, while a routine manual worker is twice as likely to be a union member than a National Trust member. Membership of the National Trust has more than quadrupled since 1980. Over the same time, period membership of trade unions has more than halved. These changes reflect a growing inequality in participation. Some people – particularly the middle classes – are participating more than ever, while for others – especially the working classes – participation in civic life in all its forms has declined immensely – and these are the same people who have dropped off the electoral radar.

The benefits to society of the bonds created by social networks and voluntary associations – 'social capital' in the academic jargon – are immense. High levels of social capital have been linked to well-functioning government, better health and education, lower crime rates and even lower levels of tax evasion. In Britain, while some groups are more engaged than ever, others are dropping out of public life altogether, weakening the social bonds that help make society function. The growing inequality in participation is not just a problem for politicians trying to interest voters in the next election, it is a problem for us all.

FURTHER READING

The seminal work on the importance of social capital is Robert Putnam's *Bowling Alone* (Simon & Schuster, 2000). For analysis of social capital in Britain see 'Social Capital in Britain' by Peter Hall (*British Journal of Political Science*, 1999) and for a recent update see 'The uneven distribution and decline of social capital in Britain' by Lindsay Richards and Anthony Heath (Centre for Social Investigation Briefing Note 15, 2015). For more detail on how social influences affect political participation see 'Why People Vote: Estimating the Social Returns to Voting' by Alan Gerber et al. (*British Journal of Political Science*, 2016).

'The enemy isn't conservatism. The enemy isn't liberalism. The enemy is bullshit.'

LARS-ERIK NELSON

—CHAPTER 39—

Who would Santa Claus vote for? The polarisation of politics

Will Jennings

Just before Christmas 1998, a Fox News/Opinion Dynamics poll of US voters found that 9 per cent thought Santa Claus would consider himself a Democrat and just 6 per cent a Republican. The vast majority – 62 per cent – believed he would be an independent. It was a time where little love was lost between the parties, as Congress prepared to impeach President Clinton over the Monica Lewinsky scandal, a political feud which divided the nation largely on party lines. With both sides hurling lurid charges back and forth, few people thought that Santa would identify with the antics of either American party.

Move forward to December 2015, when YouGov asked a similar question, and things had changed. Now more Americans thought Santa would pick a party, with 23 per cent saying Santa would be a Democrat, 13 per cent a Republican. The share saying Santa would be an independent had dropped nearly twenty points to 46 per cent. Santa, it seems, has joined the political fray.

THE PARTISAN IDENTIFICATION OF SANTA CLAUS 1998 AND 2015

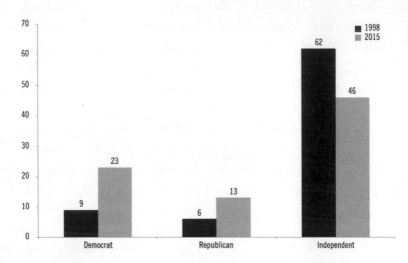

The change in responses to this festive survey question is sympto-
matic of a long-term shift among the American electorate towards
worldviews increasingly dominated by partisanship. Even Jesus does
not escape; in another US poll 82 per cent of Democrats thought that
Jesus would support stricter gun laws, while 67 per cent of Republicans thought he would oppose them.

In Britain, too, there is evidence of similar partisan differences.
In a YouGov poll from 2013, some 27 per cent said Father Christ-
mas would vote Labour, 23 per cent for Green, and 17 per cent for
the Tories, while 13 per cent thought Father Christmas would back
UKIP – and as a white, older man, he does fit the bill (although Ukip-
pers are often not keen on foreign workers who show little regard for
British border controls). A poll in 2016 on fictional characters and
Brexit found that voters thought the Vicar of Dibley, Sir Humphrey
Appleby and Mary Poppins would vote to Remain in the EU, whereas
Catherine Tate's Nan, Basil Fawlty and Jim Royle would be for Out.

America's growing political polarisation is often characterised as a 'culture war' between Red and Blue America, with 'filter bubbles' reinforced by the politicisation of cable news and, more recently, social media – where people are less and less exposed to information and opinions with which they disagree. An increasing number of Democrat and Republican identifiers hold negative views of the other party, and of its supporters.

Certainly, Republican and Democrat identifiers have become more consistently ideological in their opinions. Survey evidence from the Pew Research Center shows that the 'average' Republican is now more conservative than nine out of ten Democrats, while the average Democrat is more liberal than roughly the same proportion of Republicans – where the figure twenty years ago was closer to seven out of ten. This widening ideological gap between the parties is interlinked with the gradual extinction of conservative Democratic and moderate Republican politicians: more partisan candidates encourage more partisan voting, and more partisan voting in turn further encourages more partisan candidates.

Something similar is happening in England too, with research showing a growing divide in public opinion between 'Two Englands' – in the widening gap between urban cosmopolitan areas that are global in outlook, liberal and more plural in their sense of identity, and declining, end-of-the-line towns that are more inward-looking, relatively illiberal, negative about Europe and immigration, nostalgic and more English in their identity. This schism translates into partisan support, with Labour faring better in urban cosmopolitan constituencies in the 2015 general election, but the Conservatives streets ahead in the hinterland.

Survey evidence in the US also shows that partisan antipathy has grown, with the percentage of partisans holding very unfavourable views of the opposing party more than doubling in the last two decades (and as Chapter 16 shows, such partisan hostility can divide families in Britain too). On top of this, the majority of those expressing a strong dislike for the opposing party also see them as posing 'a threat to the nation's well-being'. Mutual anger and distrust have become the motives driving many partisans' views of each other, and of politics as a whole. In England, too, about the only thing that unifies cosmopolitan and provincial voters is their distrust of mainstream politics.

However, not all the evidence paints such a tribal picture. While Republicans and Democrats as a specific group have polarised, the US electorate as a whole has not. Indeed, the number of Americans who self-identify as independents is close to record levels – which is not what you might expect at a time of ideological division – just as in the UK the percentage of people strongly identifying with a party has fallen. The noisiest voices in the political discussion are not necessarily the most representative, even if they are heard now more than ever.

Some argue that polarisation is not because people's views on issues and ideology have become more strongly divided, but because such views are now more consistently aligned with their partisan identity – a process known as 'partisan sorting'. American voters are spread from left to right overall in much the same way as they always were. But the opinions of each party's supporters have become both more consistent with other supporters, and more distinct from supporters of the opposition. In short, the parties overlap less than they used to. Republicans now hold more consistently conservative positions with greater regularity, while Democrats are more reliably liberal in their opinions. Instead of the electorate having split into liberal and conservative blocs, the parties (and their supporters) have become more internally homogenous and distinct from each other.

But politics never stands still, and this long-running sorting process may be shifting once again. Recently, large sections of many parties' traditional support base have begun defying their ruling elites. In America, the rise of the Tea Party, the nomination of Donald Trump as the GOP candidate for President in 2016 and support for Bernie Sanders among some Democrats – fuelled by anti-establishment sentiment and distrust – reveal cracks in party unity on both sides. In Britain, the rise of Jeremy Corbyn and the success of UKIP in part reflect similar internal fissures. This fracturing may even save Santa: the 2015 polling on Santa's partisan sympathies suggests a decline in partisan sorting since a peak in 2012. While there may currently be Two Americas or Two Englands – with a different Santa for each – this state of affairs may not last forever if the surge in anti-politics sentiment breaks up the existing duopoly.

FURTHER READING

The Pew Research Center report, *Political Polarization in the American Public* (2014), sets out survey evidence regarding the growing ideological consistency of partisans and dislike of the other party. Morris Fiorina's *Culture War? The Myth of a Polarized America* (Pearson, 2010) highlights the trend of 'partisan sorting' that leads the parties to become more homogenous. Will Jennings and Gerry Stoker discuss the polarisation of public opinion in the context of British politics in 'The Bifurcation of Politics: Two Englands' (*Political Quarterly*, 2016), suggesting that such trends may not be unique to America.

CHAPTER 40

The heavenly chorus's upper-class accent: compulsory voting and public policy

Lukas Schmid

Voter turnout has been decreasing in most democracies since World War Two. This trend alarms many observers who consider low turnout a threat to the legitimacy of policymaking. They also worry that because voting and other forms of political participation are dropping, money begins to matter more in politics, and politicians target policies to those – typically richer and higher-educated – individuals that turn out to vote. American researcher E. E. Schattschneider captured such anxieties long ago when he wrote: 'The flaw in the pluralist heaven is that the heavenly chorus sings with a strong upper-class accent.'

One possible solution is compulsory voting: if everyone is legally obliged to vote, politicians will have to take into account the views of the whole electorate. But would election outcomes really look different if we had virtually universal turnout? Answering that seemingly straightforward question is harder than it looks. To assess how turnout changes the results, we would ideally observe an election twice, once under high and once under low turnout. This is, of course, impossible. Alternatively, we could simply measure the preferences of citizens who do not vote and predict how political outcomes would change if they went to the polls. But this overlooks that compulsory voting might change parties' policy platforms and mobilisation campaigns as they tailor their effort to cater to the new voters.

Switzerland provides a way around this methodological problem. Or more specifically, federal referendums in Switzerland in the first half of the twentieth century, when the twenty-five different cantons all voted on the same proposals, but did so using different voting rules. The canton of Vaud practised compulsory voting for about twenty years, between 1925 and 1948. In most other cantons, however, voting remained voluntary. Switzerland in this period therefore gives us a natural experiment allowing us to observe the same referendum under high and low turnout.

In Vaud citizens who abstained had to pay a substantial fine of two Swiss francs (roughly an hour's wage for a blue-collar worker) that was collected by the local police. The fine boosted turnout by thirty percentage points—giving Vaud participation rates of around 90 per cent.

Consistent with the idea that fining non-voters mobilises citizens with low income the most, compulsory voting increased the support for leftist, redistributive policy, for example bills that proposed stricter market regulation and expanded welfare programmes. The figure below shows the evolution of support for leftist policy proposals for districts in Vaud (solid line) and districts in the control cantons (dotted line). The dots are calculated based on twenty-four federal leftist policy proposals between 1908 and 1948. The grey shaded area represents the period in which Vaud practised compulsory voting.

THE EFFECT OF COMPULSORY VOTING
ON SUPPORT FOR LEFTIST POLICY

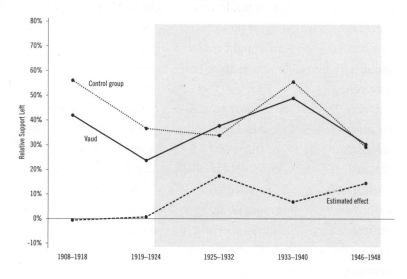

Districts in Vaud were less supportive of leftist policy proposals compared to districts in the control cantons in the period before Vaud
introduced a fine for failing to vote in 1925. But as soon as authorities in Vaud introduced compulsory voting, electoral support for
leftist policy increased by about eight to fifteen percentage points
when compared to the cantons where there was no fine. The dashed
line in the figure shows the difference in support for leftist policies
between districts in Vaud and districts in the control cantons, adjusted
for their pre-existing differences before the introduction of compulsory voting. This adjustment is necessary to make districts in Vaud
comparable to other districts in terms of their pre-compulsory voting support for leftist policies.

To illustrate the impact of the surge in turnout, look at two policy proposals that were particularly relevant in the first half of the
twentieth century. The first is the so-called 'crisis initiative' in 1935,

to fight the effects of the Great Depression. It stipulated a large set of leftist policy reforms, including a state guarantee for a minimum wage, subsidies to workers and farmers, higher unemployment benefits and stricter regulation of financial markets. Compulsory voting increased support for the crisis initiative in Vaud by around twenty-two percentage points compared to the level of support in the absence of compulsory voting. As it was, this achieved a vote share of 42.8 per cent across all of Switzerland, with voting only mandatory in Vaud. A comprehensive compulsory voting scheme for all Swiss citizens could have easily tipped the balance in favour of this ambitious initiative, with major consequences for public policy. As another example, consider the popular initiative to introduce the right to work in 1947. Here, electoral support for this policy was a massive thirty percentage points higher in Vaud than it would have been without compulsory voting. This proposal achieved a 31 per cent yes share nationwide, another result that indicates that nationwide mandatory voting might have changed the final national result.

So, low turnout may indeed lead to policy choices that reflect the views of those who vote, at the expense of those who are politically underrepresented. But the Swiss experience also helps us deal with the concern that compulsory voting mobilises uninformed voters who will vote almost randomly, because it shows very little increase in wasted ballots. Less than 6 per cent of those who are mobilised by compulsory voting issue a blank or invalid ballot paper. The prompt abolition of mandatory voting in 1948 also allows us to explore whether this long-standing mandatory voting rule changed citizens' voting habits. Immediately after Vaud abolished compulsory voting, turnout declined to levels equal to those in the control cantons. This suggests that, contrary to other research suggesting voting is a lasting habit, many voters in Vaud found it easy to quit the polls when they no longer faced a fine for staying at home on election day.

FURTHER READING

More information about the effects of compulsory voting on public policy can be found in Bechtel et al.'s 'Does Compulsory Voting Increase Support for Left Policy?' (*American Journal of Political Science*, 2016), and the long-term effects of compulsory voting are discussed in 'Compulsory Voting, Habit Formation, and Political Participation' (2016) by the same authors. A study of the adoption of compulsory voting in Australia, which finds similar results for election outcomes, is Anthony Fowler's 'Turnout Matters: Evidence from Compulsory Voting in Australia' (*Quarterly Journal of Political Science*, 2013). Schattschneider's heavenly chorus quote comes from his *The Semisovereign People* (1960).

—CHAPTER 41—

A demographic time bomb: the right and ethnic diversity

Nicole Martin

E thnic minority electorates are causing headaches for right-wing party strategists across Europe and North America. Ethnic minorities are on average younger than the rest of the population and, with a few exceptions, tend to vote reliably for left-wing parties. As minority electorates grow, they will pose a growing, perhaps existential, challenge for parties of the right: how to appeal to ethnic minority voters, without alienating white voters who are sceptical of immigration and multiculturalism?

The loyalty of ethnic minority voters to left-wing parties is so strong that some have termed it an 'Iron Law'. But it is not a blind or unthinking loyalty. In Europe, left-wing parties have usually been the first to put forward ethnic minority candidates, and tend to have more minority representatives. Although trade unions were initially hostile to minorities – supporting white workers who did not want to work with black workers – left-wing parties have generally been more welcoming of immigrants, and pioneered anti-discrimination laws that helped ethnic minorities access better housing and jobs.

Perhaps most importantly, as ethnic minorities become a greater

227

share of the electorate, they also make up an increasing share of left-wing parties' supporters. In 2010, ethnic minorities were 21 per cent of Labour voters, but just 5 per cent of Conservative ones. To put the figures another way, there were about four and a half times more ethnic minority Labour voters than Conservative ones in 2010. Reliable data on 2015 is harder to come by, but what data we have suggests a similar pattern.

The association between ethnic minority voters and left-wing parties is also present in a wide range of countries with very different political systems. In the 2012 US presidential election, 93 per cent of black and 71 per cent of Latino voters supported Barack Obama, in contrast to just 39 per cent of white voters (as discussed further in Chapter 43). Just before the 2013 German federal elections, 50 per cent of Turkish voters expected to vote for the Social Democrat Party, who went on to win only 29 per cent of the vote of the wider electorate. In the Netherlands, the association is so strong that one Dutch council was forced to redesign its strategy to increase ethnic minority turnout when its opponents pointed out that this would almost only benefit the governing left-wing party.

However, many right-wing politicians take comfort in the notion that ethnic minority voters will switch to the right as racial prejudice declines, and second- or later-generation voters find themselves in middle-class jobs, surrounded by high-achieving white voters who lean right. The British Conservative Party has been trying to reach out to south Asian voters since the 1970s – considering these voters to be a natural constituency due to their conservative social values and high rates of small business ownership. They cite recent increases in support from Indian and Pakistani voters as evidence that such a strategy is starting to pay dividends. The German right-wing Christian Democrats similarly increased their vote among ethnic Turkish voters at the 2013 federal elections. Meanwhile in Canada, the Conservatives convinced many minority voters to break their loyalty to the Liberals by the 2010 elections. As the ethnic minority electorate is increasingly made up of the native-born children of immigrants, rather than their parents, who faced more discrimination on arrival and tend to be employed in working-class occupations, minority voters have become more similar to right-wing white voters: more middle-class, more suburban, wealthier.

However, a cautionary tale from the US should sober those who assume that ethnic minority voters will slowly but surely desert the left as they move into middle-class suburbia. In 1996, 74 per cent of Asian Americans supported the Republican candidate Bob Dole. By 2012 this had reversed, with Obama winning 73 per cent of the Asian-American vote. The reason? Current Republican hostility to immigrants sits uneasily with Asian-American voters. Despite on average having higher earnings, Asian Americans face prejudice and discrimination just as other minorities do. The problem for right-wing parties is that often their leadership expresses attitudes and promotes policies that are popular with white voters, for example those worried about immigration, but which do not sit well with minority voters – something very evident in the 2016 primary campaigns of Republican candidates Donald Trump and Ted Cruz.

The Canadian Conservatives' success in winning over minority voters was achieved by highly targeted policies at specific immigrant groups – such as lifting certain visa restrictions or apologising for a past levy that was only applied to Chinese immigrants – yet when facing defeat in the 2015 election, the party's representatives once again succumbed to the temptation to play to white voters' anxieties, putting forward a number of anti-Muslim policies. This did not save them on polling day, and squandered the minority voter goodwill they had worked hard to build up. Indeed, it is not just right-wing parties that harm their appeal to ethnic minority voters in this way. The German Social Democratic Party (SPD) discovered this to their cost in 2010, when Berlin's former finance minister published a book called (in translation) 'Germany Does Itself In' in which he claimed that German Muslims rely too much on social services, and are of lower intelligence. Although the book struck a chord with many white voters, it damaged the SPD's standing among Muslim voters. This is the paradox parties face: they cannot easily respond to white voters' concerns over immigration and identity without antagonising rapidly growing ethnic minority electorates.

So ethnic diversity is a challenge for parties in general, but right-wing parties in particular, who start at a disadvantage with minority voters. How can such parties win the trust of ethnic minority voters while also retaining white voters uneasy with social change? One option may simply be to wait. Later generations of ethnic minority voters, who have faced less racial prejudice than their parents, access middle-class jobs and do not associate the centre-right as strongly with racism and xenophobia, may be more willing to give such parties a hearing. For the same reasons, the left cannot take ethnic minority loyalty for granted. Parties of the left will still retain many minority voters, not least because we tend to learn our politics from our parents – but as the ethnic minority electorate diversifies in experiences and attitudes, right-wing parties will find an opportunity developing.

FURTHER READING

For an overview of ethnic minority political behaviour in Great Britain see *The Political Integration of Ethnic Minorities in Britain* (Oxford University Press, 2013), by Heath et al. Rob Ford and others explain the difficulties of measuring vote shares among minority populations, and estimate what happened in 2015, in 'Are the Conservatives really breaking through with ethnic minority voters?' (YouGov, 2015). For research that shows diversity of political opinion among Germany's immigrant-origin ethnic minorities, see Kroh and Tucci's 'The Party Identification of Germany's Immigrant Population: Parties Should Not Fear Eased Naturalisation Requirements' (2010).

'There is no time for vacations during a campaign.'

ATTRIBUTED TO QUINTUS TULLIUS CICERO, 64BC

—CHAPTER 42—

The politics of the past in the present: Poland's electoral geography

Ben Stanley

There are lots of spurious correlations out there. Swimming pool drownings per year correlate with the number of films starring Nicolas Cage. Murders by hot objects correlate with the age of Miss America. Civil engineering doctorates awarded correlate with the per capita consumption of mozzarella cheese. So when a map circulated on social media showing a close correspondence between levels of support for the candidates in Poland's presidential election of 2010 and the extent of the Polish rail network in 1952, the statistically savvy observer could be forgiven for assuming that this was simply another striking coincidence.

In one sense, it is. Rail networks do not *cause* someone to vote for a particular candidate – a few voters' choices might get swung by the building of a branch line or the renovation of an old station, but elections don't turn on such things. Yet apparent coincidences of geography can provoke us to think more systematically about the relationships between historical legacies and present-day behaviour. Poland's rail network provides us with a good illustration of this.

Between 1795 and 1918, Poland did not exist as a sovereign state. What is now modern-day Poland was divided between three occupying imperial powers: the kingdom of Prussia in the north and west, the Russian empire in the east and centre, and the Austrian empire in the south. The occupying powers varied both in the resources they devoted to these regions and in their attitudes to the local Polish population. The Prussians invested in industrialisation and the development of infrastructure (hence the more extensive rail network), but suppressed Polish culture and identity through a programme of Germanification. The Russians were even more repressive of Polish identity, without the compensation of economic and social development. The Austrians did not suppress Polish national identity, and even permitted the Polish population a degree of self-government, but their partition remained impoverished and largely rural.

After Poland regained independence in 1918, the volatility of party politics and the increasingly uncompetitive nature of elections meant that the legacies of partition had only a limited effect on outcomes. Then after World War Two, there followed nearly half a century of communist rule, in which egalitarian indoctrination was supposed to have rendered citizens of communist countries incapable of perceiving economic and social differences, while repression of religious beliefs and institutions and the promotion of alternative historical narratives should have severed the threads of cultural continuity with the past.

Yet, despite these efforts, the distant past is still present in contemporary Polish politics. In the lands of the former Prussian partition, voters lean towards the more liberal, cosmopolitan and pro-European Civic Platform (PO), while in the areas of the former Russian partition and – particularly – the former Austrian partition, the conservative, nationalist and Eurosceptic Law and Justice (PiS) has generally had the upper hand, particularly in more rural areas. This pattern has been observed in successive parliamentary and presidential elections since 2005, when these two parties came to prominence.

And while we should be careful to avoid committing the ecological fallacy, making inferences about the behaviour of individual voters on the basis of aggregate patterns, studies from individual-level analyses produce exactly the same finding. Voters who live in the post-Russian and post-Austrian regions are more likely to support PiS and less likely to support PO, while those in the post-Prussian region are more likely to support PO and less likely to support PiS, even when controlling for a range of important determinants of party choice.

Yet while the past is present, it is not necessarily decisive, nor are all of its legacies of equal importance. One study found that the economic legacies of partition are not as significant as generally assumed. Across the border of the former Prussian and Russian partitions, changes in support for PO and PiS are gradual in character – a smooth change, not a 'jump'. This helps explain why in 2015 PiS was able to make significant inroads into PO's more economically prosperous western heartlands even while the line of partition still remained visible on the overall map of voting behaviour. On the other hand, sharper differences remain at the border between the former Russian and Austrian partitions. Levels of religiosity 'jump' on the Austrian side, as do levels of support for the religious-conservative PiS, while support for the liberal PO decreases significantly. The greater persistence of the cultural legacy of partition is in keeping with the most consistent finding of the literature on post-transition Polish voting behaviour: Poles' votes are driven by cultural values first, with economic interests secondary (or even irrelevant).

All maps are simplifications, particularly the ones which reach us as internet memes. The temptation to search for patterns can be misleading: colour-coded plots of constituency-level support can suggest that there are stark and substantial differences where there are actually myriad shades of grey. Nevertheless, these simplifications serve a purpose. When patterns of socio-economic and cultural phenomena overlap with spatial distributions of political support, something important is often going on. Some of the striking patterns we see on maps have obvious roots in the recent past, such as votes cast for the far-left *Die Linke* in regions of the former East Germany, or Labour electoral strongholds around coal fields in the UK. Others, such as the correlation between support for UKIP and residence in seaside towns, may not immediately provide us with an obvious explanation. Still others, such as the relationship between support for Donald Trump and the propensity to conduct internet searches for racial epithets, may tempt us to draw superficial conclusions. Yet as the Polish case shows, they may also draw our attention to more complex explanations we might otherwise have neglected to investigate.

FURTHER READING

An accessible account of the impact of historical legacies on the emergence of a 'Liberal Poland' versus 'Solidaristic Poland' cleavage can be found in '"The Past Is Never Dead": Identity, Class, and Voting Behavior in Contemporary Poland', by Krzysztof Jasiewicz (*East European Politics & Societies*, 2009). Irena Grosfeld and Ekaterina Zhuravskaya's analysis of 'spatial discontinuities' in 'Cultural vs. Economic Legacies of Empires: Evidence from the Partition of Poland' is a more challenging read, but despite the technical jargon is not inaccessible to the lay reader (*Journal of Comparative Economics*, 2015). Tomasz Zarycki's 'History and Regional Development: A Controversy over the "Right" Interpretation of the Role of History in the Development of the Polish Regions' provides a useful summary of the debate over how to interpret the legacies of partition in light of present-day Polish politics (*Geoforum*, 2007). For further examples of spurious correlations, see Tyler Vigen's *Spurious Correlations* (Hachette Books, 2015).

—CHAPTER 43—

Is demography destiny?
America's changing electorate

Shaun Bowler

The US is changing fast. The share of the population and of the electorate who are white is dropping while the share of other racial
and ethnic groups is growing. As the graph shows, the proportion
who are white fell from 76 per cent in 1990 to 65 per cent in 2010;
it is predicted to be just 60 per cent by 2020. On current trends, by
2044 the US will no longer be majority white.

These demographic changes present a series of challenges to some of
the ways in which we think about political behaviour, which are typically
based on research which focuses on the white majority. For example, the
conventional understanding of political participation is that social attrib-
utes, especially education and income, are drivers of participation: the
better off and the better educated take part more because they have
the resources – financial and/or cognitive – to be able to do so. This tends
to be much less true for Asian Americans, who, on average, have levels
of income and education that should be associated with high political
participation, but, as a group, currently participate much less than we
would expect from our models. At the same time, African Americans
participate more than we would expect from income and education levels.

CHANGING COMPOSITION OF THE US POPULATION 1990–2020

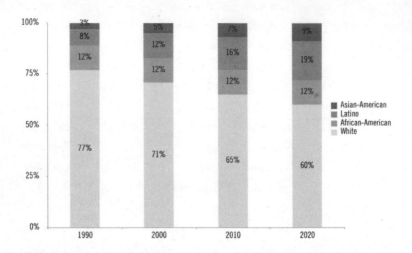

One possibility is that differences in participation relate – at least somewhat – to immigrant status (as discussed in Chapter 25). Many Asian Americans are first-generation immigrants, and immigrants are often uncertain how to participate in their new home. Many may be fleeing regimes in which political participation was not seen as a good thing, or may prefer to avoid drawing potentially hostile attention to themselves. Yet this lower-than-expected participation persists even for many second (or more)-generation Asian Americans.

One influential line of argument emphasises how people are socialised into political attitudes from a very early age. Many people who immigrate did not grow up in their new home country, and so missed out on this socialisation process. How immigrants acquire attitudes and what attitudes they acquire are therefore interesting questions whose answers provide insight into, and amend our understanding of, processes of socialisation. The first generation of immigrants seems to have much more positive views of democracy and the US system of government than do those who have been brought up in the US. First-generation Latinos, for example, come to the US seeing the political system in very positive and supportive terms, often more positive than US-born whites. Successive generations, however, develop much gloomier views. This is identical to the process seen with non-white immigrants into the UK.

A third puzzle presented by changing US demographics is over the nature of identity politics. Social identities are powerful ways in which people see themselves and are seen in relation to society. In the US case, an especially important argument has been that of linked or shared fate. This argument, developed in relation to African-American experience but applied in recent scholarship to both Latinos and Asian Americans, holds that people have a set of shared histories and experiences, which lead them to consider themselves as part of a wider group and not just as individuals: injuries to individuals from a group are seen as injuries to the wider community as well. Where racial and ethnic identities overlap and are homogenous, then identities, and identity politics, may be clear-cut. In some ways that kind of identity politics makes it possible to talk of vote blocs such as 'the African-American vote'. Over the past generation, rising intermarriage between different racial and ethnic groups means that roughly 3 per cent of the US population now see themselves as 'multi-racial' – and that group is growing fast. This group of people prompts some rethinking about identity politics.

These demographic changes also obviously matter to politicians because, as the electorate changes, so too do the electoral calculations they need to make. This is clearest in relation to the rapid rise in the Latino and Asian-American populations of the US, predicted to be almost 30 per cent of the overall population by 2020. Roughly speaking, Latino populations are largest in the southwest and west, Asian populations biggest in the west. Latinos comprise over 30 per cent of the population in four states: Arizona, California, New Mexico and Texas. For those familiar with the game of constructing electoral coalitions using the building blocks of social groups, this means that for many states a new vote bloc has to be considered and won over, or a bigger bloc needs more attention than previously. In many ways, the interests of these blocs of voters – schools, jobs, housing – are the same as any other bloc. But there are differences and distinctions. For example, immigration policy is an especially important concern to Latino voters. At the same time, while affirmative action policies resonate as a remedy for discrimination for African-American voters, Asian-American voters are often less supportive of such policies, especially with regard to areas such as university admissions. Candidates and campaigns, then, have to be careful how to address these issues and be more sensitive to issues of race and ethnicity as the electorate grows ever more diverse.

Historically, much of American politics has been 'about' race and this isn't going to change soon. Candidates have to be more mindful about the policies they stand for and the words and images they use in their campaigns. As a simple example, English-language ads in English-language news sources are no longer the only means of carrying a campaign message. While the fundamentals of electoral politics – organising, campaigning, voting – remain the same, the content of US politics will change in the coming century. It will be a century of new voices being heard.

FURTHER READING

The literature on the politics of the changing US population is growing fast. One broad overview source is Bowler and Segura's *The Future Is Ours* (CQ Press, 2011). But many other sources exist, notably McClain and Stewart's excellent *Can We All Get Along?* (Westview Press, 2014). On linked fate specifically, see the work of Michael Dawson in his *Behind the Mule: Race and Class in African-American Politics* (Princeton University Press, 1994). The Pew Research Center provides current data and studies on US Latinos and has begun to provide information on the US Asian-American population. Other groups include the AAAJ (Asian Americans Advancing Justice) or UCLA's Asian American Studies Centre.

CHAPTER 44

Electing one of our own? Ireland's personal politics

Michael Marsh

Election campaigns are not remote events in Ireland. Most Irish voters have a direct experience of elections, typically by having their doorbell rung by a candidate. Irish Election Studies report well over half of those who voted say that someone called to their home during the campaign. For most, this means at least one candidate visited; and for almost a quarter, more than one candidate visited the house around election time. A large majority of those surveyed also reported in one study that they had spoken to the candidate they voted for, 21 per cent saying they had spoken 'often' and a further 27 per cent reporting they had done so 'occasionally', with another 23 per cent saying 'once or twice'. This is a remarkable level of personal contact with politicians, much higher than in almost all other comparable countries.

This type of contact matters. A visit by a candidate increases by around 50 per cent (depending on the party) the likelihood that a voter will back the candidate's party, and vote for the candidate who is making the contact in particular.

Partly, this is the result of Ireland's unusual electoral system, a multi-member per constituency procedure that allows voters to choose between multiple candidates from the same party; the result is intensified and personalised competition, especially within the larger parties.

Then there's the relatively small scale: constituencies are a little smaller than those in the UK, and each elects between three and five members to the Dáil (Irish Parliament), so a successful candidate might need to win fewer than 10,000 votes. That is a manageable number of households to visit, even in the three weeks of a normal campaign (and of course real campaigning happens over a longer period than that).

Personal contact also works because it is what Irish voters want from their politicians: surveys consistently reveal an Irish electorate that wants its politicians to have strong roots in the constituency, and to spend a substantial amount of their time on constituency-related business, dealing with the problems of groups and individuals, and doing what they can to bring more state benefits to their constituency – and often their particular neighbourhood within it. For voters, and those outside Dublin in particular, having a TD (Teachta Dála – Irish MP) from the local area is rated as important as having one who shares one's opinions. Even in 2011, with the economic crisis at its peak, most voters thought that TDs devoted almost half of their time to local matters, but still felt they should devote even more.

Ireland is far from unique in having members of its national parliament representing a constituency and working hard on its behalf. The difference is that most Irish TDs – particularly outside Dublin – have deep roots in their constituency: they live there, so did their parents, and they have widespread and long-standing involvements in local organisations. A significant number have parents who were also local representatives, and until it was prohibited more than ten years ago, most also sat on local councils. Voters know their candidates are local, and know most devote a lot of time to local matters. It is seen as a fundamental characteristic of Irish politics.

And yet this conception of Irish politics, generally ridiculed by broadsheet commentators if defended by politicians and valued by voters, is in some respects a caricature. Voters do value their local candidate, but the party label under which that candidate stands is not irrelevant. Exit polls have asked voters in recent years which is the most important factor in their choice: picking a Taoiseach (prime minister), a set of ministers, a set of policies, or a candidate to serve to needs of the constituency. Yes, more than 40 per cent each time have chosen the last of these and yes, it was the most popular option – but a majority picked a national factor, whether policies or leadership. Irish Election Studies have similarly asked whether or not voters would have chosen the same candidate had they been running under a different party label, and while most say they would not, a significant number would have done so, or said that it would depend on the party.

THE MOST IMPORTANT CRITERION NAMED BY IRISH VOTERS IN DECIDING HOW TO VOTE

	2007	2011	2016
NATIONAL			
The Taoiseach	12	7	10
The set of ministers that will form the government	23	13	14
The policies as set out by the parties	25	43	34
LOCAL			
A candidate to look after the needs of the constituency	40	38	43
Total	100	100	100

Source: RTÉ exit polls 2007, 2011, 2016. Figures may not add up to 100 due to rounding.

Clear patterns of support based on locality are striking, but this is particularly true in the larger parties running more than one candidate, and in part reflects the large parties' efforts to manage support in this way so as to maximise their chances of winning extra seats. In reality it is too simple to see most voters as picking a candidate or a party, as for many the decision is a balance of these things.

However, it is clear that the prominence of localism affects how parties behave. They select candidates with a keen eye to local prominence. Relatives of a former TD for a constituency are often seen as ideal as they combine known partisanship with a strong recognition factor in local networks. 'Parachuting' candidates into a constituency where they have no local connections is virtually unknown.

So is this a solution for Britain's much maligned politicians? Almost certainly not. For one thing, one of the results of this is a weak parliament, which is particularly subservient to government. There is relatively little incentive for a TD to address themselves to national policy-making rather than local service, and most do not. Calls for parliamentary reform are growing and the new parliament elected in February 2016 will certainly be more active, and maybe more constructive.

Moreover, trust in political institutions remains low. Irish people were no more trusting in their national parliament than were voters of EU countries as a whole over the last few years, both before and after the economic crisis, with mistrust particularly severe at the height of 'austerity'. There is, for sure, evidence that they like *their* TDs (as discussed in Chapter 27). But the 2011 Irish Election Study found that politicians in general were seen as pretty untrustworthy – on a par with journalists. In 2016 an Irish Election Studies survey found 'most politicians' continued to be seen as untrustworthy. It may be nice to have a neighbour in the Dáil, but when tough decisions have to be made, governments, even in Ireland, can look very remote.

FURTHER READING

Maciej Gorecki and Michael Marsh's 'A Decline of "Friends and Neighbours Voting" in Ireland? Local Candidate Effects in the 2011 Irish "Earthquake Election"' (*Political Geography*, 2014) and the same authors' 'Not Just "Friends and Neighbours": Canvassing, Geographic Proximity and Voter Choice' (*European Journal of Political Research*, 2012) each try to assess the national evidence for the impact of campaign contact and localism on voting. There is a wider discussion of the roles of candidates and parties in the report of the first Irish Election Study: Michael Marsh et al.'s *The Irish Voter: The Nature of Electoral Competition in the Republic of Ireland* (Manchester University Press, 2008). The most recent election is discussed in Michael Gallagher and Michael Marsh's edited *How Ireland Voted 2016* (Palgrave Macmillan, 2017).

—CHAPTER 45—

We're all right, Jacques: blue-collar support for the French radical right

Jocelyn Evans

About twenty years ago, French political scientists first noticed that blue-collar workers (*les ouvriers*), assumed to be largely the electoral preserve of the socialist and communist parties, were voting in growing numbers for the Front National (FN). By 2015, every country with a substantial radical right party – Austria, Belgium, the Netherlands, Norway, Sweden, the UK – had apparently witnessed the same awkward trek of working-class voters across the ideological spectrum to support parties with names like the Freedom Party (Austria), the Progress Party (Norway) or the UK Independence Party, who, regardless of name, tend to a similar mix of nationalism, populist attacks on the ruling class and hostility to immigration.

The standard explanation for this defection focuses on ethnocentrism – or, in its most recent guise, anti-Muslim sentiment – and political disenchantment. There also remains a normative assumption among many politicians and commentators that such voters, unlike small business owners, the petty bourgeoisie and other, traditionally more 'naturally' right-wing social groups, are electorally somehow in the wrong place.

This blue-collar shift has changed the FN's electoral profile sociologically, making it (by definition) more working-class, and it has generally been assumed that much of the ideological baggage these new voters have brought, particularly on economic issues, has been of the left. Given the extent of this influx, which saw Marine Le Pen win the largest share of the blue-collar vote in 2012 (around 30 per cent), an obvious expectation would be that the French radical right has shifted leftwards, at least on economic issues. Such assumptions are behind questions of the sort 'Is the FN now a party of the left?' from respected organs such as *Le Figaro* and the BBC. A further assumption, recycling the 1980s protest vote narrative of radical right voting, underpins the working-class FN model – that such voters are aware of the incongruity between their economic preferences and those of their current party, and would change political channels were the mainstream left once again able to present a true left-wing alternative focused on delivering radical redistributive policies.

In reality, this neat narrative of angry blue-collar workers camping out temporarily on the radical right is simplistic. Equating voters' social profiles with parties' ideological positions is a poor idea anywhere, but particularly in France, which has a fine history of substantial working-class support for figures difficult to reconcile with the left, from General Boulanger in the 1880s to General de Gaulle in 1965. More recently, quite apart from the FN success among this demographic, around a quarter of the blue-collar vote went to the right-wing Nicolas Sarkozy in the 2007 presidential election, and five years earlier, the French working class split 50/50 across candidates of the left and of the right.

In the French case, *gaucho-* or *ouvriero-lepénisme* in fact combines blue-collar supporters from the socialists with similar supporters from the mainstream right. True defection from left to radical right is only part of the story. A symptom of this can be seen in voters' views of where their ideological 'home' is, by asking them where they see themselves on the left–right spectrum. In France, as elsewhere, left and right are regularly written off as an anachronism. But many voters still seem able to make sense of the scale and are happy to classify themselves on it. Where do those workers who support the FN and Le Pen place themselves? The graph below uses the French presidential post-election surveys from 1988 to 2012 to map these voters in comparison with other Le Pen voters and with other blue-collar voters. According to the survey, the left–right measurement changes, so the scale is standardised around a 0 centre-point, negative values indicating left-of-centre placement, positive values right-of-centre.

LEFT–RIGHT POSITIONS OF LE PEN BLUE-COLLAR VOTERS, OTHER LE PEN VOTERS AND OTHER BLUE-COLLAR VOTERS IN FRENCH PRESIDENTIAL ELECTIONS (1988–2012)

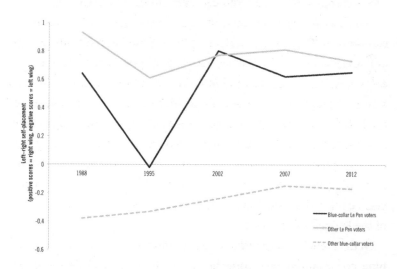

The findings make depressing reading for enthusiasts of the 'lost lefties' hypothesis. For the last quarter of a century, with one exception, blue-collar workers supporting the Le Pen family have placed themselves firmly on the political right. The exception is 1995, and perhaps expectedly so, given this was the election where the party most actively campaigned on job creation, housing and the minimum wage, playing on the recently defunct socialist executive's failures. But since then, blue-collar FN voters (black line) have occupied a position well to the right of other blue collar voters (dashed grey line). Of course, FN voters are only a minority of the working class – and those who don't vote FN tend, on the whole, to place themselves on the left. We also cannot say from this data how long they have been with the FN, or whether their left–right positioning has changed during their sojourn. What we can say is that, ideologically, since the FN's electoral breakthrough, blue-collar Le Pen voters have resembled Le Pen supporters from other social classes much more than they have their class comrades who support other parties.

In 2012, this broad political alignment of working-class Le Pen voters was corroborated by other aspects of their economic outlook. Le Pen voters were the most likely to agree with the suggestion that the unemployed could get jobs if they tried, and the blue-collar Le Pen voters were no less likely to agree that *les chômeurs* should get on their *vélo*. Le Pen voters were the most likely to agree that current tax rates were unfair, and blue-collar agreement was if anything slightly higher. For Le Pen voters, 'affluence' began at just over €5,000 per month, the lowest of any of the presidential candidates – and only working-class Sarkozy supporters estimated it lower. Such voters are more reminiscent, then, of British working-class Tories, socially and economically conservative, than of disgruntled socialists.

Of course, in France as in any post-industrial economy, the blue-collar class is a shrinking section of the workforce, relative to the larger routine non-manual class (*les employés*). The very fact that it is a shadow of its former self suggests that its economic and ideological outlook may have changed, and will continue to do so – when blue-collar FN supporters say 'things aren't like they used to be', they have a point. In a case such as France, where the electoral result of such changes is still presented as somehow out of phase with 'normal' politics, we find a useful reminder that social class can encompass a range of mutually exclusive world-views.

FURTHER READING

For the first outing of *gaucho-lepénisme*, see Pascal Perrineau and Colette Ysmal's *Le Vote de crise: L'Élection présidentielle de 1995* (Presses de Sciences Po, 1995). For a more formalised model of the phenomenon, see Jocelyn Evans's 'Le Vote gaucho-lepéniste: le masque extrême d'une dynamique normale' (*Revue Française de Science Politique*, 2000) – easier than the 300-page English PhD thesis. Nonna Mayer's *Ces Français qui votent Le Pen* (Flammarion, 2002) adopts a different perspective through *ouvriero-lepénisme*. And for a definitive take on how FN economic policy may well have evolved in line with its electorate, see Gilles Ivaldi's 'Towards the Median Economic Crisis Voter? The New Leftist Economic Agenda of the Front National in France' (*French Politics*, 2015). The author thanks Nicolas Sauger for kindly providing the 2012 survey data for this analysis.

CHAPTER 46

Bart De Wever's weight in chips: governing without a government

Chris Terry

Bart De Wever is the Mayor of Antwerp, in Flanders, in the North of Belgium. He is also the leader of the New Flemish Alliance, a centre-right Flemish separatist party. He was once rather rotund, though recent dieting has made him much trimmer.

Bart De Wever's weight is significant, because during the Belgian coalition negotiations that took place for a world record 541 days between June 2010 and December 2011, the Flemish youth radio station Studio Brussel ran a sweepstake on when Belgium would get a government. The winner would receive De Wever's weight in Belgium's national dish: chips. The winner, announced on 2 December 2011, won 100 traditional (and large) Belgian cones of chips. That's a lot of chips.

The reasons for this lengthy period without a government are rooted in the delicate relations between Belgium's French- and Flemish-speaking communities, who make up 40 and 60 per cent of the population respectively.

For much of Belgium's history the French speakers dominated politically and economically, with French the only official language on Belgium's formation in 1830. Thus began a long Flemish struggle for political equality, which reached its completion in the 1960s.

Around the same time, two significant events occurred. First, Belgium's three major parties – the Christian Democrats, the Socialists and the Liberals – split into separate Flemish and Francophone parties. Belgium now has no major party which runs in both Francophone and Flemish areas.

Secondly, Wallonia, the French-speaking south, lost its traditional economic advantage over Flanders as its industrial economy went into decline just as Flanders began to take advantage of the emerging service economy.

In Flanders, a Flemish nationalist movement had always been present, but in 2010 the New Flemish Alliance became the largest party in Belgium. Flemish and Francophone parties took increasingly polarised positions. Belgian governments have to involve parties from both communities, but after 2010 there was very little the two communities' main parties could agree on. The result was no government, for a very long time. Belgium's experience helps answer the question: what happens when a country doesn't have a government?

During periods of election or coalition negotiation, countries, including Belgium and Britain, are typically governed by a so-called caretaker government. This is usually made up of members of the outgoing administration, but without the 'full' powers of an elected government. Such an administration is usually barred from carrying out major policy changes. A country needs some kind of government to carry out the day-to-day small stuff, or to deal with major crises or international incidents. After the 2010 UK election, European finance ministers were invited to a summit on the eurozone. This was before the coalition deal between the Conservatives and Liberal Democrats. So Alistair Darling, the Brown government's Chancellor of the Exchequer, represented Britain, though he also had agreement from his eventual successor, George Osborne, on what terms could be agreed.

Belgians are much more used to caretaker administrations than the

British, as coalition wrangling is a well-established part of their political process, so most were rather unconcerned as negotiations stretched on and on. The caretaker administration not only continued to govern, but made some fairly significant decisions. Over its 541 days in office, it negotiated a budget, joined the international military intervention in Libya, participated in eurozone rescue programmes, bailed out and nationalised banks and spent six months holding the rotating Presidency of the EU. Not bad for a government no one had (quite) elected!

In a period when governments across Europe were beginning to tighten their belts, Belgium's not-quite-a-government imposed an odd, passive, kind of not-quite-austerity. Expensive new policy initiatives could not be started. Public sector wages were effectively frozen and the ability to hire new staff was also curtailed. Doing very little can be an effective way to save money.

Belgians showed no sign of being particularly bothered by their lack of a formal government. There were no public protests. Why are the Belgians so comfortable with a protracted vacuum at the top? One reason is that what outsiders see as 'the government' is in fact only the top tier of a complex layer cake, and for most Belgians, most of the time, it is not the tier they care about most. Belgium is a complicated federal state, with wide-ranging powers devolved to regional and community governments. The latter, for instance, run educational policy, while the regional governments are so powerful that they can sign foreign trade deals independently of the federal government.

Despite caretaker finance minister Didier Reynders declaring that the supposedly caretaker government could keep going all the way to the next federal elections, it was, as in Britain in 2010, external pressures that eventually forced the formation of a new government. As time went on, the piles of unsolved problems in the federal government in-tray grew ever higher. Reforms were needed to deal with Belgium's budget deficit, which not-quite-austerity proved not-quite-enough to resolve. Not having a formal government also meant a growing risk that the unelected caretakers would have to take responsibility for a major crisis situation, undermining Belgium's delicate consensus politics approach. Anxieties about all of this led to the downgrading of Belgian debt by two of the major credit-rating agencies. Belgium's political elites thus came together in December to form a government headed by Elio Di Rupo. In the end, the bond markets succeeded where voters and parties had failed.

So, the sky does not fall in when a country is without a government. Public bureaucrats continue to do their jobs. Decisions can and will be taken by caretaker administrations. It is no one's interest to see a country stop functioning, especially if there is a chance they might get the blame for it. Taxes will continue to be collected, services will continue to function and people's lives will carry on.

And eventually, external pressures will likely force the emergence of a new government. That might take 541 hours or 541 days, but inevitably the day will come when the costs of failing to cooperate become too large, even for deeply divided political elites. Then, if you're lucky, you might just win Bart De Wever's weight in chips.

FURTHER READING

For more on Belgium's experience of governing without a government, see 'Governing without a Government: The Belgian Experiment' by Carl Devos and Dave Sinardet in *Governance* (2012) and on the reasons behind the lengthy coalition negotiations of 2010–11 see 'The Political Crisis in Belgium (2007–2011): A Federal System without Federal Loyalty' (*Representation*, 2012). *The Politics of Coalition: How the Conservative–Liberal Democrat Government Works* by Robert Hazell and Ben Yong (Hart Publishing, 2012) is a good guide to the functioning of coalition in the UK. *Working Together*, an Electoral Reform Society report edited by Chris Terry, features short articles by both domestic and international politicians about governing in a coalition context.

—CHAPTER 47—

Why buy crap when you can buy money? German party funding

Dan Hough

How should politics be funded? The question is hardly new, and a lot of (both academic and practitioner) legwork has gone into trying to find the answer. One model that periodically catches the attention of UK policy-makers is that of Germany. The German system of party funding comprises three basic elements: party members pay subscriptions; individuals and corporate bodies donate money directly; and parties that poll above 0.5 per cent of the vote in regional, national and European elections receive subsidies from the state.

As a result, parties are encouraged to recruit members to keep them rooted in society and to help fund day-to-day activities. They are also encouraged to solicit donations from individuals (and indeed corporations), but given that donors may well favour parties in (or near) government, smaller parties in particular know that they still have a degree of state support on which they can fall back. Most of the attention and debate about party funding in Germany, as in most countries, focuses on the funding methods of the large parties. Yet the behaviour of two of Germany's smaller parties illustrates that even well-thought-through systems of party finance can be made to look ridiculous.

In October 2014, for example, the Alternative for Germany (AfD), a spikey right-wing party that entered the European Parliament that year, began selling gold in its online shop. The AfD sold it in the form of gold coins (the €490 replica German Mark coin was particularly popular – it sold out within days) and gold bars. In the first eleven days of business, the party managed to persuade over 800 people to part with around €1.6 million.

The aim of the AfD's metamorphosis into a gold-selling business was twofold; first, any profits would flow directly into the party's bank account. But the party also hoped that it would be able to claim more money from the state. The party was entitled to claim around €5 million on account of the votes it received in elections, but it could only get that if it illustrated that it had raised the same amount of money by itself. If a party is unable to do this, then it only gets funds proportionate to the money that it has managed to raise. So, the more gold sold, the more money German taxpayers would need to give the AfD.

It didn't take long for a reaction to the AfD's subsidy-inducing wheeze to materialise. Protests were lodged, investigations were undertaken. The Bundestag's administration conducted a thorough enquiry into whether the AfD's behaviour contravened Germany's so-called 'Party Law'. Much to the consternation of the President of the Federal Parliament, Norbert Lammert, it didn't, and unless the law was changed then the state would have to support the AfD's gold-selling antics.

Inspired by the AfD, Die Partei (literally 'The Party') came up with an even more left-field wheeze. Die Partei is a German version of the Monster Raving Loony Party, well known for coming up with schemes and ideas that are aimed at making others look silly. So we perhaps shouldn't have been surprised when it announced that if the AfD could sell gold, then it could sell cash. Or, as the party itself chose to put it, 'Why go round buying crap, when you can buy money?'

Die Partei announced that for €105 you could buy €100; for €25, you'd get €20. Much to Die Partei's surprise, this scheme swiftly saw German citizens spend €80,000 on buying money, at a loss. Given that 'The Party' was entitled to claim up to €240,000 in subsidies from the state (as it polled 0.6 per cent in the European Parliament election of 2014), the German taxpayer found, much as with the AfD, that he/she was subsequently compelled to match every cent of the money-selling in the form of matched subsidies.

The sight of Germans ruthlessly applying rules with absurd effect is in and of itself mildly amusing, but these cases also tell us a little more about what we should and should not expect from party-funding debates. The German party-funding regime is short on neither laws nor judicial attempts to interpret them, but that hasn't saved it from two parties trying to play the game. That in late December 2015 the German authorities ultimately changed the rules explicitly to prevent incoming funds such as these from being eligible for matching state subsidies is not the point.

Party-funding regimes never stand still, as rational actors do their level best to game existing rules to their best advantage, although usually parties do tend to try to avoid attracting public attention when doing so. Furthermore, normative assumptions about what is and what isn't appropriate behaviour will differ considerably. For some the AfD and Die Partei were chancers bringing the system into disrepute; for others they were simply quicker and more nimble than their bigger, more established opponents, or performing a public service by exposing flaws in the existing rules. While the AfD and Die Partei made the German system look decidedly silly, similar absurdities could happen with pretty much any funding regime, given that all the possible ways of funding politics are to some extent flawed. Sharp-eyed politicians will, perhaps understandably, make these flaws work to their advantage whenever they can.

FURTHER READING

For general background on debates on German party funding see Susan E. Scarrow's 'Beyond the Scandals? Party Funding and the 2005 German Elections' (*German Politics*, 2006). For more on German politics more broadly see Simon Green et al.'s *The Politics of the New Germany* (Routledge, 2011), and for more on how the German authorities changed the party-funding law on account of the AfD's behaviour see 'After the gold rush: AfD loses state subsidies' (*Deutsche Welle*, 2015).

—CHAPTER 48—

Women must die! Gender in Japan

Tina Burrett

Japan is dying. The 2015 national census reports that the country's population shrank by almost one million in just five years. The National Institute of Population and Social Security Research predicts that Japan will lose one-third of its 127 million people by 2060. The ratio of Japanese citizens sixty-five or older will surge to 40 per cent from the current 24 per cent during the same period. Children under fifteen account for just 13 per cent of the overall population, the lowest share among countries with populations of at least 40 million. Japan's fertility rate, at 1.4 in 2014, is well below replacement level. In rural Japan, schools are closing, while the nursing home industry is booming.

This rapid demographic decline is taking its toll on the once mighty Japanese economy. In 1995, Japan's gross national income accounted for 15 per cent of the world's total. It will fall to 5.2 per cent in 2050 and to a mere 1.7 per cent in 2100 if the current trend continues. To maintain the nation's population and restore its economic prowess, Japan's Prime Minister, Shinzo Abe, announced in April 2013 that he wanted to create a society in which women 'shine' (using the English word), making 'womenomics' an essential part of his 'Abenomics' economic growth strategy.

There's plenty of room for improvement. No Nikkei 225 company is run by a Japanese woman, and only 1.5 per cent of Japan's most senior executives are women, compared to 40 per cent in Norway and 28 per cent in France. In September 2013, Abe announced lofty plans to boost the number of women in senior executive positions to 30 per cent by 2020. But Japan's corporate and cultural norms prevent women from meeting their full potential in the workplace. The practice of recruiting new graduates into 'jobs for life' makes it difficult for women to take career breaks or to find new positions when returning to work after raising families. About 70 per cent of Japanese women leave the workforce after giving birth.

Raising Japan's gender equality would not only improve opportunities for women, but could also bring significant economic benefits. Equal participation in the workforce would tackle Japan's labour shortage by adding eight million women to the labour market, potentially increasing GDP by up to 20 per cent over the next two decades, according to the OECD.

There is also little evidence of women shining in Japanese politics. Only 8 per cent of Japan's lower-house parliamentarians are female, placing Japan 129th in global league tables of female political empowerment, below Saudi Arabia and Syria.

And despite his promises, Prime Minister Abe has done very little practically to promote gender equality, devoting more energy to downplaying Japan's treatment of Korean sex slaves – euphemistically known as 'comfort women' – during World War Two, than to empowering 21st-century women. Abe's lack of commitment to gender equality is not surprising, as he has previously supported redrafting the Japanese constitution to privilege 'traditional values' over universal human rights. During his first administration in 2007, Abe's Health Minister Hakuo Yanagisawa referred to women as 'birth-giving machines', arguing that if more women stayed home they would produce more babies, and thus more future workers.

Chauvinistic attitudes remain pervasive in Abe's Liberal Democratic Party (LDP), undermining government efforts to help women 'shine'. In June 2014, female legislator Ayaka Shiomura suffered sexist sneers from LDP colleagues about her single, childless status as she addressed the Tokyo Metropolitan Assembly about childcare and fertility issues. In January 2016, LDP politician Kensuke Miyazaki shook up the conservative establishment by becoming the first Japanese lawmaker to take paternity leave. But it was soon revealed that he was using his time away from the office for a tryst with a bikini model, just days before his wife, a fellow LDP parliamentarian, gave birth. Abe's 'pink' reshuffle in September 2014, which saw a record-equalling five women promoted to his cabinet, backfired when two female ministers were quickly forced to resign due to campaign finance irregularities – scandals which were leaked by male colleagues resentful at being passed over for promotion. In any case, women have been offered second-tier cabinet positions, rather than key ministries like foreign affairs or finance. Even when Abe appointed a woman, Yuko Obuchi, to the trade and industry portfolio for a short period, she was prevented from taking part in the Trans-Pacific Partnership (TPP) trade negotiations.

Even the name of Prime Minister Abe's much-trumpeted 'shine' initiative came with an unfortunate twist. The word 'shine', when pronounced in Japanese (*shee*-nay), means 'die'! 'Women must die!' was not, we can assume, the sentiment Abe's initiative meant to convey.

Such a call for patriotic self-sacrifice, even if intended, would meet stiff resistance from Abe's fellow citizens: Japanese women are in fact less willing to die for their country than women of practically every other nation. The *World Values Survey* found that only 9 per cent of its women would fight for Japan in a war, while globally, an average of 54 per cent of women and 69 per cent of men would make the ultimate patriotic sacrifice. On this question, Japan compares particularly unfavourably with its east Asian neighbours.

WOULD YOU BE WILLING TO FIGHT FOR YOUR COUNTRY?
(PERCENTAGE OF WOMEN RESPONDENTS ANSWERING 'YES')

GLOBAL AVERAGE	JAPAN	CHINA	TAIWAN	SOUTH KOREA	GERMANY
54	9	69	78	52	30

Source: World Values Survey 2010–2014, http://www.worldvaluessurvey.org. Respondents were asked: We all hope that there will not be another war, but if it were to come to that, would you be willing to fight for your country?

In China – locked in simmering territorial tensions with Japan – 69 per cent of women would fight for their country. In Taiwan, the figure is 78 per cent. Japan's militarism in the first half of the twentieth century perhaps accounts for why its women are reluctant to fight for the national cause. But even in Germany – with a similarly tortured historical legacy – the number of women willing to fight is 30 per cent, more than three times higher than in Japan. Japan's poor record on gender equality may offer a better explanation for Japanese women's lack of patriotic passion than lingering guilt about World War Two. Three times as many Japanese men as women would make the ultimate sacrifice.

With 'womenomics' so far amounting to little more than hollow PR, Japanese women will not be allowed to shine in the English sense of the word any time soon in politics or in the boardroom. They are therefore unlikely to sacrifice themselves for the demographic security of a country which does not value their contributions. Until that changes, Japan will continue to provide the world with an example of how male chauvinism can slowly, but surely, kill off an entire nation.

FURTHER READING

Mary Brinton's *Women and the Economic Miracle: Gender and Work in Postwar Japan* (California University Press, 1993) provides an insightful history of sex discrimination in the Japanese labour market. For an assessment of Abe's 'womenomics' policies see Helen Macnaughtan's 'Womenomics for Japan: Is the Abe Policy for Gendered Employment Viable in an Era of Precarity?' (*Asia-Pacific Journal*, 2015). Other relevant studies are Robin LeBlanc's *The Art of the Gut: Manhood, Power, and Ethics in Japanese Politics* (University of California Press, 2009) and Hiroko Takeda's 'Gender-Related Social Policy' in *The Routledge Handbook of Japanese Politics* (2011).

'A lost election can have the jolt of a drop through the gallows door, leading to a dark night of the soul in which the future presses down like a cloud that will never lift.'

JAMES WOLCOTT

—CHAPTER 49—

The people are perceptive: immigration and the EU

Geoffrey Evans

The public are often thought to be relatively ignorant about social and political issues. Even when true, this can be a little unfair. The complexity and (at times deliberate) ambiguity of many issues, and the ways they are 'spun' by the parties – keen not to be on the wrong side of a debate – often make it hard for voters to make sense of things. But there is one issue where the public has put two and two together: immigration and the EU. Actual immigration rates are the key to understanding the public's level of concern about immigration, but it's not just about the level of immigration *per se* – it's also about where people are coming from.

Immigration increased markedly at the end of the last century and has remained exceptionally high since. Public concern about immigration has closely tracked this rise in numbers (as discussed in Chapter 19). The share naming immigration as the most important issue on the political agenda rose from under 5 per cent in the mid-1990s to nearly 35 per cent in the mid-2000s. There was a dip following the onset of the economic crisis in 2007/8 – unsurprising given the magnitude of the crisis – but rising anxiety about immigration resumed soon after as the economy recovered, and is now at the highest levels on record, with 40 per cent or more naming it as the nation's most pressing issue.

In the past, the overall rate of immigration had no implications for attitudes towards the EU – as most immigrants didn't come from other European countries. In 1975, concern about immigration was high but it had no consequence for the vote to stay in the Common Market. If anything, it was the reverse: only 26 per cent of people who believed that 'too many immigrants have been let into Britain' wanted to leave the Common Market, compared with 38 per cent of those who disagreed with this statement. In 1975, anti-immigration voters decided overwhelmingly to stay in Europe.

Voters in the 1970s did not think EU membership was linked to immigration levels. Has this changed? Recent evidence separating Commonwealth, EU and 'other' sources of immigration shows that Europe looms larger in the immigration statistics than it used to. Estimates of international migration provided by the commonly used International Passenger Survey show that EU immigration played no part in the rise in immigration before 2004 – this was produced by an increase in asylum seekers, students and workers from other parts of the world. EU immigration took off with the 2004 accession of former communist-bloc countries of eastern Europe into the EU, and the government's decision not to restrict immigration from these countries during the first five years of EU membership, and thereafter EU immigration formed a major component of immigration into Britain. By 2013, it was by far the largest component, and continuing to grow as migrants from crisis-hit eurozone countries sought better opportunities in Britain.

If we compare these trends in immigration from different sources with trends in concern about immigration expressed via responses to questions about what people think are 'the most important issues facing the country' obtained from polls conducted by Ipsos MORI, we find that concern about immigration closely tracks the surge in EU immigration, but not immigration from other sources, which has been flat or falling in recent years.

In itself, however, this aggregate relationship isn't compelling evidence that individual voters are linking their attitudes to immigration with their views about the EU. To be sure, we need to look at how individual voters think about the two issues. We can examine this using a long series of monthly surveys (the Continuous Monitoring Surveys), which each month asked British voters for their views on both immigration and the EU. Using this data we can see how the link between immigration and the EU in individual voters' minds changes over time. The figure below shows the difference in EU approval scores ('How much do you approve of Britain's membership of

RELATIONSHIP BETWEEN APPROVAL OF THE EU AND CONCERN ABOUT IMMIGRATION

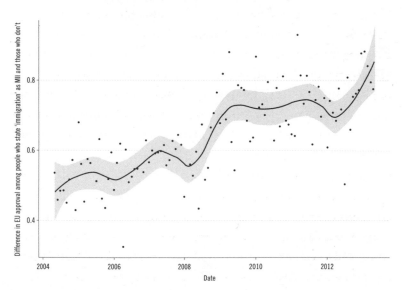

the EU?') between respondents who believe immigration is one of the most important issues facing the country, and those who don't. Each black dot represents the size of the difference in approval of the EU between people who think immigration is one of the most important issues facing the country and those who don't. The middle line is the best estimate of the position of the changing slope over time. The grey area of the graph represents the width of the confidence interval, indicating a 95 per cent probability that the true score lies within this area.

The difference in EU approval between people who believe immigration is an important problem and those who do not increases during the years following the 2004 accession before flattening off from 2009 to 2011 during the economic crisis, only to rise steeply again since 2012, as EU immigration rates also shoot upwards. Within less than a decade of the 2004 accession to the EU, concern about immigration went from being moderately distinct from approval of the EU to being strongly linked in the mind of the public.

This process had been underway for years before the Syrian refugee crisis and the closing of borders in the EU itself (which may have further strengthened it). This spiral of alarm clearly had an influence on the EU referendum vote. According to the British Election Survey, in 2015 only 10 per cent of people who did *not* believe too many immigrants have been let into the country would vote to leave the EU. But no less than 50 per cent of those who believe too many immigrants have been let in would do so. We live in a very different world to that of 1975. We have just seen the perceptive public send a message to the political establishment that is arguably unequalled in its significance. The seeds of Brexit were sown over a decade ago. Those seeds have now borne fruit in a way that Tony Blair, the chief architect of mass immigration from the EU, clearly did not foresee. The people have spoken.

FURTHER READING

For a detailed analysis of the impact of the Labour government's handling of immigration on its electoral support, see 'Explaining Voters' Defection from Labour over the 2005–2010 Electoral Cycle: Leaders, Economics and the Rising Importance of Immigration' (*Political Studies*, 2013), by Geoffrey Evans and Kat Chzhen. For a recent study of the sources and political implications of immigration and Euroscepticism in Britain, see Robert Ford and Matthew Goodwin's *Revolt on the Right: Explaining Support for the Radical Right in Britain* (Routledge, 2014). For a recent analysis of the nature of Euroscepticism see 'Are We All Eurosceptics Now?' (*British Social Attitudes*, 2015), by John Curtice and Geoffrey Evans.

CHAPTER 50

Could Jeremy Corbyn have kept Britain in the EU? The role of leadership heuristics

Matthew Goodwin

The outcome of Britain's EU referendum delivered nothing short of a political earthquake, the implications of which will be felt for decades and possibly generations to come. In the immediate aftermath Britain stood firmly apart from its European neighbours, the value of the national currency plummeted and Prime Minister David Cameron resigned. As one journalist quipped: 'It has been a rather strange day. The resignation of the Prime Minister is only our third most important story'.

Amid the national debate that followed, much of the attention focused on the role of individual party leaders. While David Cameron was criticised for taking one gamble too many, the Labour Party leader Jeremy Corbyn came under serious pressure to resign for (his MPs claimed) failing to work hard enough to mobilise the Labour-leaning Remain vote.

There was certainly evidence to support this claim. Only a few weeks prior to the result, one opinion poll by YouGov suggested that nearly one in two Labour voters did not know what the Labour Party's position was on the referendum.

During referendums and elections, citizens often turn to political leaders for guidance on how to vote. This is especially true when the vote centres on a complex issue like the EU, which excites some political activists but seldom interests most voters, who know little about it. According to a recent study which asked voters from across Europe a range of (very basic) questions about the EU, British voters were among the least knowledgeable in the Union. Only the Latvians – or the Spanish, depending on what measure you used – scored lower. Uninformed voters tend to turn to leaders they trust for guidance on what to do. Leaders thus provide what is sometimes called a 'heuristic' – an informational shortcut.

But what effect could the leaders of Britain's three most popular parties have had on the EU referendum result? An online survey experiment gives us insight into their possible impact. Some respondents were randomly assigned to be asked how they would vote at the referendum without receiving any cue, while others were instead assigned to see a recommendation from one of the party leaders – David Cameron, Jeremy Corbyn or Nigel Farage – and then asked how they would vote. While Cameron always advised a Remain vote in the experiment and Farage always advised a Leave vote, when it came to Corbyn, some respondents were told he was recommending Remain, while others were told he was backing Leave. At the time of the experiment, during the autumn of 2015, the new Labour leader was making ambivalent statements about the EU, complaining that it was 'increasingly operating like a free market'. This sparked debate about whether Corbyn, like many Labour MPs in the 1970s, was instinctively Eurosceptic and might actually recommend a Leave vote. In later months he would revise his stance and recommended that Britain remain in the EU, though to many observers he continued to appear as a reluctant passenger in the national debate.

The chart below shows the results of the experiment. The first thing to note is that in the control group, which received no steer from any party leader, the overall result was incredibly close – 51 per cent to 49 per cent – a razor-thin, two-point margin of victory for Remain. In the absence of cues from their leaders, the British voters in this sample were evenly split at this point.

SUPPORT FOR BRITAIN REMAINING IN, OR LEAVING, THE EU, DEPENDING ON PARTY LEADER STANCES

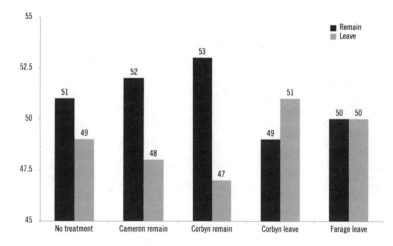

Adding in cues from political leaders changed things. First, the experiment revealed how Prime Minister David Cameron was an asset for the Remain camp. When respondents were told that Cameron recommended a Remain vote, net support for staying in the EU increased by two points. When respondents were told that Nigel Farage recommended a Leave vote, net support for staying in the EU fell by two points. What about Jeremy Corbyn? Like Cameron, a recommendation from the Labour leader to remain in the EU helped to drive net public support for this option – but by double the amount of Cameron's intervention, four points. A nudge from Corbyn to stay in the EU increased support for Remain, particularly among Labour voters, by seven points and, among 40–59-year-olds, ten points. Given evidence that nearly half of the Labour electorate did not know where Labour stood on the referendum question it suggests that had Corbyn made a more assertive, compelling and unambiguous case for Remain then the result could have been much closer, perhaps even going the other way.

But Corbyn could also persuade people in the other direction. Had Corbyn continued on his traditional Eurosceptic path and recommended a Leave vote, he could sway the electorate the other way. When respondents were told that the Labour leader was making a 'Leave' recommendation, then overall support for Brexit increased to a majority position, of 51 per cent, while support for Remain fell to 49 per cent. Much of this change came from voters in lower social classes who switched from saying they were undecided to voting to leave the EU. In the experiment, then, Jeremy Corbyn had the potential to alter the outcome of the referendum. We will never know if he could have done the same in reality.

FURTHER READING

For public attitudes towards the European Union in Britain, see the final chapter in Matthew Goodwin and Caitlin Milazzo's book *UKIP: Inside the Campaign to Redraw the Map of British Politics* (Oxford University Press, 2016). For recent work on how leadership cues can influence voter behaviour at referendums see Sara Hobolt, 'Taking Cues on Europe? Voter Competence and Party Endorsements in Referendums on European Integration' (*European Journal of Political Research*, 2007). On low voter knowledge about the European Union see the summary of research by Simon Hix ('Britons among least knowledgeable about European Union') on the Guardian's datablog (2015).

'Politics is supposed to be the second oldest profession. I have come to realise that it bears a very close resemblance to the first.'

RONALD REAGAN

—CHAPTER 51—

Happiness and a penis: politics and sexual satisfaction

Joe Twyman

I t was at lunch with the American ambassador that Yvonne de Gaulle, wife of General Charles de Gaulle, was asked what she was looking forward to most about her husband's impending retirement. 'A penis,' she is reported to have replied. In response to the ensuing stunned silence, her husband, so the story goes, leant over and said, 'My dear, I think it's pronounced "happiness".'

It was not the first time sex, politics and happiness were linked in conversation, nor would it be the last. The caricature of the frigid, unimaginative, sexually awkward Tory gets an airing with some regularity, particularly within the Westminster bubble – all thick pyjamas, separate beds and general unhappiness. Conservative both in and out of the bedroom is the label hung around their neck, in contrast to those sexually liberated, carnally contented Liberals and Labour lefties, all body hair and coital contortions.

There is certainly evidence that Labour and Conservative supporters have different sex lives. Labour supporters are, for example, significantly more likely to indulge in a much wider range of possible fantasies than Conservatives. But are they more or less satisfied as a result?

Measuring happiness is a surprisingly complicated business. But a good place to start is in southern Asia. The country of Bhutan at the eastern end of the Himalayas has, since 1971, measured its population's Gross National Happiness (GNH) as an alternative to Gross Domestic Product (GDP). This is derived from survey data asking the population a series of questions about their happiness including 'Taking all things together, how happy would you say you are?'

Ask this question to a nationally representative study of over 14,000 British adults (the same ones as in Chapter 24), with respondents recording their answer on a scale ranging from 0 (Not at all) to 100 (Very happy), and the mean is 67 out of 100. Using the same scale, ask 'Generally speaking, how happy would you say you are with your sex life?' for those who said they were currently sexually active in a previous question, and the mean was 70. Madame de Gaulle might not have been surprised to discover that the two correlated strongly (albeit at 0.43 not *very* strongly).

And in contrast to the most popular Westminster stereotypes, among the supporters of different political parties it was Conservatives and UKIP supporters who had the highest levels of sexual happiness, above the national average, while Labour, Lib Dem and supporters of other parties were marginally lower, although the differences were not large on the whole.

The differences became slightly larger – but still not all that substantial – when it came to general life happiness, but while Conservatives topped that table too, Ukippers shared the bottom with Labour and other voters.

Another way to analyse these results is to break them down by where respondents place themselves on the left–right political ideology scale. This data was recorded in the survey using standard question wording and on a scale from 0 (Left) to 100 (Right). Those who see themselves as very left-wing (scoring 0–20) were the least happy with their life in general (averaging 62). General happiness then increased, as we move along the left–right scale: 65 for those who were left-wing (21–40), 67 for those in the centre (41–60), 70 for those on the right (61–80) and 71 for those on the far right (81–10). The relationship with sexual happiness isn't quite as strong, but those on the right do, again, seem to report higher levels of sexual happiness than those on the left (a mean of 73 for those scoring 80–100, compared to 68 for those scoring 0–20).

The advantage of breaking the data down by ideological placement like this is that it allows for a relatively straightforward comparison between different countries. YouGov also polled the same questions in four other northern European countries, and as the table below shows, the left are consistently the least lucky in lust. In all five countries surveyed, it was the people giving themselves a score that placed them in the 'Very right-wing' group who reported the highest levels of sexual happiness. In Britain, Denmark and Sweden that same group were also the happiest in general terms too. Those placing themselves on the centre-left were least happy with their sex lives in four of the five countries (the exception being de Gaulle's France, where the centre-right are least happy, despite the best efforts of Nicolas Sarkozy). When it comes to general happiness, it is the far left who are most discontented everywhere except, once again, France.

SEXUAL HAPPINESS

	ALL ADULTS	VERY LEFT WING	LEFT WING	CENTRE	RIGHT WING	VERY RIGHT WING
Britain	70	68	66	71	70	73
Germany	72	71	73	72	72	77
France	71	69	69	72	67	75
Denmark	72	70	69	73	71	75
Sweden	69	68	66	71	70	73

GENERAL HAPPINESS

	ALL ADULTS	VERY LEFT WING	LEFT WING	CENTRE	RIGHT WING	VERY RIGHT WING
				LEFT–RIGHT PLACEMENT		
Britain	67	62	65	67	70	71
Germany	63	62	62	63	66	62
France	61	65	63	59	57	61
Denmark	72	69	70	72	75	75
Sweden	67	62	65	67	70	71

Obviously there are numerous factors that might explain both an individual's self-reported sexual happiness and their general life happiness – and the old rules about correlation and causation always apply. It is not suggested that being very right-wing makes you happier in bed (or on the stairs, on the kitchen floor, in the shower and on the backseat of the car).

But in contrast to at least one broad stereotype, it is those on the right of the political spectrum who enjoy their sex life the most – across a number of different countries – and indeed enjoy life in general more. Perhaps this is more in line with an alternative stereotype of critical, sexless left-wingers?

FURTHER READING

For insight into the sexual fantasies of different party supporters, see the chapters by Joe Twyman and Bernadeta Wilk in *Sex, Lies and the Ballot Box* (Biteback, 2014). For more on the intricacies of measuring happiness in Bhutan see 'Gross National Happiness in Bhutan: A Living Example of an Alternative Approach to Progress' by Alejandro Adler Braun (*Social Impact Research Experience Journal*, 2009).

Bibliography

Adler Braun, Alejandro, 'Gross National Happiness in Bhutan: A Living Example of an Alternative Approach to Progress', *Social Impact Research Experience Journal* (2009) [http://repository.upenn.edu/sire/1/]

Allen, Nicholas and Birch, Sarah, *Ethics and Integrity in British Politics: How Citizens Judge their Politicians' Conduct and Why It Matters* (Cambridge: Cambridge University Press, 2015)

Allen, Peter, Cutts, David and Campbell, Rosie, 'Measuring the Quality of Politicians Elected by Gender Quotas – Are They Any Different?', *Political Studies* (2014) [Available early online]

Ansolabehere, Stephen and Iyengar, Shanto, *Going Negative: How Political Advertising Shrinks and Polarizes the Electorate* (New York: Free Press, 1995)

Association of Electoral Administrators, 'Elections and Individual Electoral Registration – The Challenge of 2015' [http://www.aea-elections.co.uk/wp-content/uploads/2015/07/aea-report-elections-and-ier-challenge-of-2015.pdf] (July 2015)

Balsom, Denis, Madgwick, P. J. and van Mechelen, Denis, 'The Red and the Green: Patterns of Partisan Choice in Wales', *British Journal of Political Science* (1983), vol. 13, no. 3, pp. 299–325

Bara, Judith, 'A Question of Trust: Implementing Party Manifestos', *Parliamentary Affairs* (2005), vol. 58, no. 3, pp. 585–99

Beaman, Lori, Duflo, Esther, Pande, Rohini and Topalova, Petia, 'Female Leadership Raises Aspirations and Educational Attainment for Girls: A Policy Experiment in India', *Science* (2012), vol. 335, no. 6068, pp. 582–6

Bechtel, Michael M., Hangartner, Dominik and Schmid, Lukas, 'Compulsory Voting, Habit Formation, and Political Participation', working paper (2016)

— —, 'Does Compulsory Voting Increase Support for Left Policy?', *American Journal of Political Science* (2016) [Available early online]

Bélanger, Éric and Meguid, Bonnie M., 'Issue Salience, Issue Ownership and Issue-Based Vote Choice', *Electoral Studies* (2008), vol. 27, no. 3, pp. 477–91

Bennett, W. Lance and Sergerberg, Alexandra, *The Logic of Connective Action* (Cambridge: Cambridge University Press, 2013)

Berg, Joyce, Nelson, Forrest and Rietz, Thomas, 'Prediction Market Accuracy in the Long Run', *International Journal of Forecasting* (2008), vol. 24, no. 2, pp. 285–300

Berglund, Frode, Holmberg, Sören, Schmitt, Hermann and Thomassen, Jacques, 'Party Identification and Party Choice' in Thomassen, Jacques (eds), *The European Voter* (Oxford: Oxford University Press, 2005), pp. 106–123

van Biezen, Ingrid, Mair, Peter and Poguntke, Thomas, 'Going, Going... Gone? The Decline of Party Membership in Contemporary Europe', *European Journal of Political Research* (2012), vol. 51, pp. 24–56

Bimber, Bruce, Flanagin, Andrew and Stohl, Cynthia, *Collective Action in Organizations* (Cambridge: Cambridge University Press, 2012)

Bowler, Shaun and Segura, Gary, *The Future Is Ours* (Washington, D.C.: CQ Press, 2011)

Brinton, Mary C., *Women and the Economic Miracle: Gender and Work in Postwar Japan* (California: California University Press, 1993)

British Election Study, 'Westminster Impact: BES Insights into 2015' [http://www.britishelectionstudy.com/bes-resources/westminster-impact-bes-insights-into-2015/#.VoQpnZMrKAw] (2015)

Broughton, David and ten Napel, Hans-Martien (eds), *Religion and Mass Electoral Behaviour in Europe* (London and New York: Routledge, 2000)

Butler, Judith, *Undoing Gender* (New York and London: Routledge, 2004)

Campbell, Rosie and Cowley, Philip, 'Rich Man, Poor Man, Politician Man:

Wealth Effects in a Candidate Biography Survey Experiment', *British Journal of Politics and International Relations* (2014), vol. 16, no. 1, pp. 56–74

Campbell, Rosie and Heath, Oliver, 'Do Women Vote for Women Candidates? Attitudes towards Descriptive Representation and Voting Behaviour in the 2010 British Election', *Politics and Gender* (forthcoming)

Citrin, Jack, Levy, Morris and Wright, Matthew, 'Multicultural Policy and Political Support in European Democracies', *Comparative Political Studies* (2014), vol. 47, no. 11, pp. 1531–57

Clarke, Harold D. and McCutcheon, Allan L., 'The Dynamics of Party Identification Reconsidered', *Public Opinion Quarterly* (2009), vol. 73, no. 4, pp. 704–28

Clarke, Harold D., Sanders, David, Stewart, Marianne C. and Whiteley, Paul, *Political Choice in Britain* (Oxford: Oxford University Press, 2004)

Clarke, Harold D., Sanders, David, Stewart, Marianne C., Twyman, Joe and Whiteley, Paul, *Austerity and Political Choice in Britain* (London: Palgrave Macmillan, 2015)

Clements, Ben, *Religion and Public Opinion in Britain* (Basingstoke: Palgrave Macmillan, 2015)

Committee on Standards in Public Life, *Political Party Finance: Ending the Big Donor Culture* (Thirteenth Report, CM 8208) (London: HMSO, 2011)

Committee on Standards in Public Life, *Survey of Public Attitudes towards Conduct in Public Life 2012* [https://www.gov.uk/government/publications/public-attitudes-survey-2012] (September 2013)

Cowley, Philip, 'Why Not Ask the Audience? Understanding the Public's Representational Priorities', *British Politics* (2013), vol. 8, no. 2, pp. 138–63

Cowley, Philip and Ford, Robert (eds), *Sex, Lies and the Ballot Box* (London: Biteback, 2014)

Cowley, Philip and Kavanagh, Dennis, *The British General Election of 2015* (Basingstoke: Palgrave Macmillan, 2016)

Curtice, John, 'A Return to Normality? How the Electoral System Operated' in Geddes, Andrew and Tonge, Jonathan (eds), *Britain Votes 2015* (Oxford: Oxford University Press, 2015), pp. 25–40

Curtice, John and Evans, Geoffrey, 'Are We All Eurosceptics Now?', *British Social Attitudes* (2015), vol. 32, pp. 1–18

Cutts, David, Childs, Sarah and Fieldhouse, Edward, '"This is What Happens When You Don't Listen": All-Women Shortlists at the 2005 General Election', *Party Politics* (2008), vol. 14, no. 5, pp. 575–95

Dahlgreen, Will, 'Left-Wingers Like to Keep It in the Family' [https://yougov.co.uk/news/2016/02/10/left-wingers-keep-family/] (10 February 2016)

Dawson, Michael C., *Behind the Mule: Race and Class in African-American Politics* (Princeton, NJ: Princeton University Press, 1994)

Dennison, James and Goodwin, Matthew, 'Immigration, Issue Ownership and the Rise of UKIP', *Parliamentary Affairs* (2015), vol. 68, s. 1, pp. 168–87

Denver, David and Bochel, Hugh, 'A Quiet Revolution: STV and the Scottish Council Elections of 2007', *Scottish Affairs* (2007), vol. 61, no. 1, pp. 1–17

Deutsche Welle, 'After the gold rush: AfD loses state subsidies' [http://www.dw.com/en/after-the-gold-rush-afd-loses-state-subsidies/a-18928520] (18 December 2015)

Devos, Carl and Sinardet, Dave, 'Governing without a Government: The Belgian Experiment', *Governance* (2012), vol. 25, no. 2, pp. 167–71

Dolan, Kathleen, 'Voting for Women in the "Year of the Woman"', *American Journal of Political Science* (1998), vol. 42, no. 1, pp. 272–93

Dunleavy, Patrick, 'Electing the London Mayor and Police Commissioners in England and Wales: How to Use Your Two Votes Well' [http://blogs.lse.ac.uk/politicsandpolicy/electing-a-mayor-and-police-commissioners-in-england-and-wales/] (4 May 2016)

Durose, Catherine, Richardson, Liz, Combs, Ryan, Eason, Christina and Gains, Francesca, '"Acceptable Difference": Diversity, Representation and Pathways to UK Politics', *Parliamentary Affairs* (2013), vol. 66, no. 2, pp. 246–67

Edwards, Rick, *None of the Above* (London: Simon & Schuster, 2015)

Eisinga, Rob, te Grotenhuis, Manfred and Pelzer, Ben, 'Weather Conditions and

Voter Turnout in Dutch National Parliament Elections, 1971–2010', *International Journal of Biometeorology* (2012), vol. 56, no. 4, pp. 783–6

Electoral Commission, *Delivering Democracy: The Future of Postal Voting* (London: The Electoral Commission, 2004)

Electoral Reform Society, 'English Local Elections 2011' [https://www.electoral-reform.org.uk/sites/default/files/2011-English-Local-Elections.pdf] (24 May 2016)

Electoral Reform Society, 'Working Together' [http://www.electoral-reform.org. uk/blog/working-together] (24 March 2015)

Erikson, Robert S. and Wlezien, Christopher, 'Are Political Markets Really Superior to Polls as Election Predictions?', *Public Opinion Quarterly* (2008), vol. 72, no. 2, pp. 190–215

— —, 'Markets vs. Polls as Election Predictors: An Historical Assessment', *Electoral Studies* (2012), vol. 31, no. 3, pp. 532–9

— —, *The Timeline of Presidential Elections: How Campaigns Do (and Do Not) Matter* (Chicago: University of Chicago Press, 2012)

Evans, Geoffrey and Chzhen, Kat, 'Explaining Voters' Defection from Labour over the 2005–2010 Electoral Cycle: Leaders, Economics and the Rising Importance of Immigration', *Political Studies* (2013), vol. 61, s. 1, pp. 138–57

Evans, Jocelyn, 'Le Vote gaucho-lepéniste: le masque extrême d'une dynamique normale', *Revue Française de Science Politique* (2000), vol. 50, no. 1, pp. 21–51

Fenno Jr., Richard F., *Home Style: House Members in their Districts* (London: Longman, 1978)

— —, 'If, as Ralph Nader Says, Congress is "the Broken Branch", How Come We Love Our Congressmen So Much?' in Ornstein, Norman J. (ed), *Congress in Change* (New York: Praeger, 1975), pp. 277–87

Finifter, Ada W., 'Dimensions of Political Alienation', *American Political Science Review* (1970), vol. 64, no. 2, pp. 389–410

Fiorina, Morris P., Abrams, Samuel J. and Pope, Jeremy C., *Culture War? The Myth of a Polarized America* (New York: Pearson, 2010)

Fisher, Justin, Cutts, David, Fieldhouse, Edward and Rottweiler, Bettina,

'Constituency Campaigning at the 2015 General Election', paper presented at the Elections, Public Opinion & Parties Specialist Group Conference, Cardiff (2015)

Fisher, Justin, Fieldhouse, Edward and Cutts, David, 'Members Are Not the Only Fruit: Volunteer Activity in British Political Parties at the 2010 General Election', *British Journal of Politics and International Relations* (2014), vol. 16, no. 1, pp. 75–95

Fisher, Justin and vanHeerde-Hudson, Jennifer, 'Parties Heed (with Caution): Public Knowledge of and Attitudes to Party Finance in Britain', *Party Politics* (2013), vol. 19, no. 1, pp. 41–60

Fisher, Justin, Van Heerde, Jennifer and Tucker, Andrew, 'Does One Trust Judgement Fit All? Linking Theory and Empirics', *British Journal of Politics and International Relations* (2010), vol. 12, no. 2, pp. 161–188

Fisher, Stephen D., Heath, Anthony F., Sanders, David and Sobolewska, Maria, 'Candidate Ethnicity and Vote Choice in Britain', *British Journal of Political Science* (2015), vol. 45, no. 4, pp. 883–905

Ford, Robert and Goodwin, Matthew, *Revolt on the Right: Explaining Support for the Radical Right in Britain* (London: Routledge, 2014)

Ford, Robert, Janta-Lipinski, Laurence and Sobolewska, Maria, 'Are the Conservatives really breaking through with ethnic minority voters?' [https://yougov.co.uk/news/2015/06/12/are-conservatives-really-breaking-through-ethnic-m/] (12 June 2015)

Forsythe, Robert, Nelson, Forrest, Neumann, George R. and Wright, Jack, 'Anatomy of an Experimental Political Stock Market', *American Economic Review* (1992), vol. 82, no. 5, pp. 1142–61

Fowler, Anthony, 'Turnout Matters: Evidence from Compulsory Voting in Australia', *Quarterly Journal of Political Science* (2013), vol. 8, no. 2, pp. 159–82

Franceschet, Susan, Krook, Mona Lena and Piscopo, Jennifer (eds), *The Impact of Gender Quotas* (Oxford: Oxford University Press, 2012)

Gallagher, Michael and Marsh, Michael (eds), *How Ireland Voted 2016* (Basingstoke: Palgrave Macmillan, 2017)

Gauja, Anika, 'The Individualisation of Party Politics: The Impact of Changing

Internal Decision-Making on Policy Development and Citizen Engagement', *British Journal of Politics and International Relations* (2015), vol. 17, no. 1, pp. 89–105

Gerber, Alan, Huber, Gregory A., Doherty, David and Downling, Conor M., 'Why People Vote: Estimating the Social Returns to Voting', *British Journal of Political Science* (2016), vol. 46, no. 2, pp. 241–64

Gomez, Brad T., Hansford, Thomas G. and Krause, George A., 'The Republicans Should Pray for Rain: Weather, Turnout and Voting in US Presidential Elections', *Journal of Politics* (2007), vol. 69, no. 3, pp. 649–63

Goodwin, Matthew and Milazzo, Caitlin, *UKIP: Inside the Campaign to Redraw the Map of British Politics* (Oxford: Oxford University Press, 2016)

Gorecki, Maciej and Marsh, Michael, 'A Decline of "Friends and Neighbours" Voting" in Ireland? Local Candidate Effects in the 2011 Irish "Earthquake Election"', *Political Geography* (2014), vol. 41, pp. 11–20

— —, 'Not Just "Friends and Neighbours": Canvassing, Geographic Proximity and Voter Choice', *European Journal of Political Research* (2012), vol. 51, no. 3, pp. 563–82

Green, Donald, Palmquist, Bradley and Schicker, Eric, *Partisan Hearts and Minds* (New Haven, CT: Yale University Press, 2002)

Green, Jane, 'A Test of Core Vote Theories: The British Conservatives, 1997–2005', *British Journal of Political Science* (2011), vol. 41, no. 4, pp. 735–64

Green, Simon, Hough, Dan and Miskimmon, Alister, *The Politics of the New Germany* (London: Routledge, 2011)

Greenberg, Stan, *America Ascendant* (New York: Thomas Dunne Books, 2015)

Greer, Scott (ed), *Devolution and Social Citizenship in the UK* (Chicago: University of Chicago Press, 2009)

Grosfeld, Irena and Zhuravskaya, Ekaterina, 'Cultural vs. Economic Legacies of Empires: Evidence from the Partition of Poland', *Journal of Comparative Economics* (2015), vol. 43, vol. 1, pp. 55–75

Hall, Peter, 'Social Capital in Britain', *British Journal of Political Science* (1999), vol. 29, no. 3, pp. 417–61 van Haute, Emilie and Gauja, Anika, *Party Members and Activists* (London: Routledge, 2015)

Hayden Phillips Review, *Strengthening Democracy: Fair and Sustainable Funding of Political Parties* (London: HMSO, 2007)

Hazell, Robert and Yong, Ben, *The Politics of Coalition: How the Conservative–Liberal Democrat Government Works* (Oxford and Portland, OR: Hart Publishing, 2012)

Heath, Anthony F., Fisher, Stephen D., Rosenblatt, Gemma, Sanders, David and Sobolewska, Maria, *The Political Integration of Ethnic Minorities in Britain* (Oxford: Oxford University Press, 2013)

Heath, Oliver, 'Policy Representation, Social Representation, and Class Voting in Britain', *British Journal of Political Science* (2015), vol. 45, no. 1, pp. 173–93

Henderson, Ailsa, Jeffery, Charlie and Liñeira, Robert, 'National Identity or National Interest: Scottish, English and Welsh Attitudes to the Constitutional Debate', *Political Quarterly* (2015), vol. 86, no. 2, pp. 265–74

Henderson, Ailsa, Jeffery, Charlie and Wincott, Daniel (eds), *Citizenship after the Nation State: Regionalism, Nationalism and Public Attitudes in Europe* (Basingstoke: Palgrave Macmillan, 2014)

Henderson, Ailsa, Jeffery, Charlie, Wincott, Daniel and Wyn Jones, Richard, 'Reflections on the Devolution Paradox: A Comparative Examination of Multilevel Citizenship', *Regional Studies* (2013), vol. 47, no. 3, pp. 303–22

Henn, Matt, Weinstein, Mark and Forrest, Sarah, 'Uninterested Youth? Young People's Attitudes towards Party Politics in Britain', *Political Studies* (2005), vol. 53, no. 3, pp. 556–78

Hix, Simon, 'Britons among least knowledgeable about European Union' [http://www.theguardian.com/news/datablog/2015/nov/27/brits-least-knowledgeable-european-union-basic-questions] (27 November 2015)

Hobolt, Sara, 'Taking Cues on Europe? Voter Competence and Party Endorsements in Referendums on European Integration', *European Journal of Political Research* (2007), vol. 26, no. 2, pp. 151–82

Holmes, Mary, *What is Gender? Sociological Approaches* (London: Sage, 2007)

Hooghe, Marc, 'The Political Crisis in Belgium (2007–2011): A Federal System without Federal Loyalty', *Representation* (2012), vol. 48, no. 1, pp. 131–8

Horrie, Chris and Chippendale, Peter, *Stick It up Your Punter! The Uncut Story of the Sun Newspaper* (London: Heinemann, 1990)

Issenberg, Sasha, *The Victory Lab* (New York: Broadway Books, 2012)

Ivaldi, Gilles, 'Towards the Median Economic Crisis Voter? The New Leftist Economic Agenda of the Front National in France', *French Politics* (2015), vol. 13, pp. 346–69

Iyengar, Shanto, Sood, Gaurav and Lelkes, Yphtach, 'Affect, not Ideology: A Social Identity Perspective on Polarisation', *Public Opinion Quarterly* (2012), vol. 73, no. 3, pp. 405–31

Jacobson, Gary C., 'How Do Campaigns Matter?', *Annual Review of Political Science* (2015), vol. 18, pp. 31–47

Jacquet, Jennifer, *Is Shame Necessary?* (London: Allen Lane, 2015)

Jasiewicz, Krzysztof, '"The Past Is Never Dead": Identity, Class, and Voting Behavior in Contemporary Poland', *East European Politics & Societies* (2009), vol. 23, no. 4, pp. 491–508

Jefferys, Kevin, *Politics and the People: A History of British Democracy since 1918* (London: Atlantic, 2007)

Jennings, Will, 'Wrong about Nearly Everything, but Still Rational: Public Opinion as a Thermostat' in Cowley, Philip and Ford, Robert (eds), *Sex, Lies and the Ballot Box* (London: Biteback, 2014), pp. 33–7

Jennings, Will and Stoker, Gerry, 'The Bifurcation of Politics: Two Englands', *Political Quarterly* (2016) [Available early online]

Jennings, Will and Wlezien, Christopher, 'The Timeline of Elections: A Comparative Perspective', *American Journal of Political Science* (2016), vol. 60, no. 1, pp. 219–33

Johnston, Ron and Pattie, Charles, 'The British General Election of 2010: A Three-Party Contest – or Three Two-Party Contests?', *Geographical Journal* (2011), vol. 177, no. 1, pp. 17–26

Johnston, Ron, Pattie, Charles and Manley, David, 'Britain's Changed Electoral

Map in and beyond 2015: The Importance of Geography', *Geographical Journal* (2016) [Available early online]

Karpf, David, *The MoveOn Effect* (Oxford: Oxford University Press, 2012)

Kaufmann, Bruno, 'The Swedish Way To Boost Voter Turnout' [http://time.com/3558705/boost-voter-turnout-sweden-america/] (5 November 2014)

Van der Kolk, Henk, Rallings, Colin and Thrasher, Michael, 'The Effective Use of the Supplementary Vote in Mayoral Elections: London 2000 and 2004', *Representation* (2006), vol. 42, no. 2, pp. 91–102

— —, 'Electing Mayors: A Comparison of Different Electoral Procedures', *Local Government Studies* (2004), vol. 30, no. 4, pp. 589–608

Koß, Michael, *The Politics of Party Funding: State Funding to Political Parties and Party Competition in Western Europe* (Oxford: Oxford University Press, 2011)

Kroh, Martin and Tucci, Ingrid, 'The Party Identification of Germany's Immigrant Population: Parties Should Not Fear Eased Naturalization Requirements', *German Institute for Economic Research* (2010), vol. 6, no. 4, pp. 20–26

Lau, Richard R. and Rovner, Ivy Brown, 'Negative Campaigning', *Annual Review of Political Science* (2009), vol. 12, pp. 285–306

LeBlanc, Robin M., *The Art of the Gut: Manhood, Power, and Ethics in Japanese Politics* (Berkeley: University of California Press, 2009)

Lefevere, Jonas, Tresch, Anke and Walgrave, Stefaan, 'Introduction: Issue Ownership', *West European Politics* (2015), vol. 38, no. 4, pp. 755–60

Mac an Ghaill, Máirtín and Haywood, Chris, *Gender, Culture and Society: Contemporary Femininities and Masculinities* (Basingstoke: Palgrave Macmillan, 2007)

McClain, Paula D. and Stewart Jr., Joseph, *Can We All Get Along?* (Boulder, CO: Westview Press, 2014)

McKibbon, Ross, 'Labour dies again', *London Review of Books* (4 June 2015), vol. 37, no. 11, pp. 11–12

McLaren, Lauren, 'Immigration and Perceptions of the Political System in Britain', *Political Quarterly* (2013), vol. 84, no. 1, pp. 90–100

— —, *Immigration and Perceptions of National Political Systems in Europe* (Oxford: Oxford University Press, 2015)

Macnaughtan, Helen, 'Womenomics for Japan: Is the Abe Policy for Gendered Employment Viable in an Era of Precarity?', *Asia-Pacific Journal* (2015), vol. 13, no. 1, pp. 1–18

Mair, Peter, *Ruling the Void* (London: Verso, 2013)

Marsh, David, O'Toole, Theresa and Jones, Su, *Young People and Politics in the UK: Apathy or Alienation?* (Basingstoke: Palgrave Macmillan, 2007)

Marsh, Michael, Sinnott, Richard, Garry, John and Kennedy, Fiachra, *The Irish Voter: The Nature of Electoral Competition in the Republic of Ireland* (Manchester: Manchester University Press, 2008)

Mattes, Kyle and Redlawsk, David P., *The Positive Case for Negative Campaigning* (Chicago: University of Chicago Press, 2014)

Mattinson, Deborah, *Talking to a Brick Wall* (London: Biteback, 2010)

Mayer, Nonna, *Ces Français qui votent Le Pen* (Paris: Flammarion, 2002)

Mellon, Jon and Prosser, Chris, 'Missing Non-Voters and Misweighted Samples: Explaining the 2015 Great British Polling Miss' [http://www.britishelectionstudy. com/bes-impact/missing-non-voters-and-misweighted-samples-understanding-the-great-british-polling-miss/] (22 January 2016)

Mellon, Jonathan, 'Party Attachment in Great Britain: Five Decades of Dealignment' [http://papers.ssrn.com/sol3/papers.cfm?abstract_id=2745654] (9 March 2016)

Mitchell, James, Bennie, Lynn and Johns, Rob, *The Scottish National Party: Transition to Power* (Oxford: Oxford University Press, 2012)

Mjelde, Hilmar L., 'Non-Member Participation in Political Parties: A Framework for Analysis and Selected Examples from Scandinavia', *Representation* (2015), vol. 51, no. 3, pp. 299–310

Nadeau, Richard, Martin, Pierre and Blais, Andre, 'Attitude towards Risk-Taking and Individual Choice in the Quebec Referendum on Sovereignty', *British Journal of Political Science* (1999), vol. 29, no. 3, pp. 523–39

Nai, Alessandro and Walter, A., *New Perspectives on Negative Campaigning: Why Attack Politics Matters* (London: ECPR Press, 2015)

Naurin, Elin, *Election Promises, Party Behaviour and Voter Perceptions* (Basingstoke: Palgrave Macmillan, 2011)

Norris, Pippa and Inglehart, Ronald, *Sacred and Secular* (Cambridge: Cambridge University Press, 2004)

Norton, Philip and Wood, David M., *Back from Westminster* (Lexington: University Press of Kentucky, 1993)

Page, Benjamin I. and Shapiro, Robert Y., *The Rational Public: Fifty Years of Trends in Americans' Policy Preferences* (Chicago: University of Chicago Press, 1992)

Palan, Kay M., Areni, Charles S. and Kiecker, Pamela, 'Re-examining Masculinity, Femininity, and Gender Identity Scales', *Marketing Letters* (1999), vol. 10, no. 4, pp. 363–77

Perrineau, Pascal and Ysmal, Colette, *Le Vote de crise: L'Élection présidentielle de 1995* (Paris: Presses de Sciences Po, 1995)

Persson, Mikael, Sundell, Anders and Öhrvall, Richard, 'Does Election Day Weather Affect Voter Turnout? Evidence from Swedish Elections', *Electoral Studies* (2014), vol. 33, pp. 335–42

Pew Charitable Trusts, 'The Elections Performance Index 2012' [http://www.pewtrusts.org/en/research-and-analysis/reports/2014/04/07/the-elections-performance-index-2012] (7 April 2014)

Pew Research Center, 'Political Polarization in the American Public' [http://www.people-press.org/2014/06/12/political-polarization-in-the-american-public/] (12 June 2014)

Pike, Joe, *Project Fear: How an Unlikely Alliance Left a Kingdom United but a Country Divided* (London: Biteback, 2014)

Pinker, Steven, *The Better Angels of Our Nature* (London: Penguin, 2012)

Plutzer, Eric and Zipp, John F., 'Identity Politics, Partisanship, and Voting for Women Candidates', *Public Opinion Quarterly* (1996), vol. 60, no. 1, pp. 30–57

Political and Constitutional Reform Committee of the House of Commons, *Voter Engagements in the UK* (Fourth Report of Session 2014–15, HC 232) (London: HMSO, 2015)

Political and Constitutional Reform Committee of the House of Commons, *Voter Engagements in the UK*: follow up (Sixth Report of Session 2014–15, HC 938) (London: HMSO, 2015)

Putnam, Robert, *Bowling Alone* (New York: Simon & Schuster, 2000)

Rallings, Colin, Thrasher, Michael and Borisyuk, Galina, 'Seasonal Factors, Voter Fatigue and the Costs of Voting', *Electoral Studies* (2003), vol. 22, no. 1, pp. 265–79

Renwick, Alan, 'Don't Trust Your Poll Lead: How Public Opinion Changes during Referendum Campaigns' in Cowley, Philip and Ford, Robert (eds), *Sex, Lies and the Ballot Box* (London: Biteback, 2014), pp. 79–84

Richards, Lindsay and Heath, Anthony, 'The uneven distribution and decline of social capital in Britain', Centre for Social Investigation Briefing Note 15 (2015)

Rose, Richard, *Using Open Data to Combat Corruption* (Glasgow: University of Strathclyde Studies in Public Policy, 2015)

Rothschild, David, 'Forecasting Elections: Comparing Prediction Markets, Polls and their Biases', *Public Opinion Quarterly* (2009), vol. 73, no. 5, pp. 895–916

Royed, Terry J., 'Testing the Mandate Model in Britain and the United States: Evidence from the Reagan and Thatcher Eras', *British Journal of Political Science* (1996), vol. 26, no. 1, pp. 45–80

Sandri, Giulia and Seddone, Antonella, 'Sense or Sensibility? Political Attitudes and Voting Behaviour of Party Members, Voters, and Supporters of the Italian Centre-Left', *Italian Political Science Review* (2015), vol. 45, no. 1, pp. 25–51

Särlvik, Bo and Crewe, Ivor, *Decade of Dealignment* (Cambridge: Cambridge University Press, 1983)

Scarrow, Susan E., *Beyond Party Members* (Oxford: Oxford University Press, 2015)

— —, 'Beyond the Scandals? Party Funding and the 2005 German Elections', *German Politics* (2006), vol. 15, no. 4, pp. 376–92

Schattschneider, Elmer Eric, *The Semisovereign People* (New York: Holt, Rinehart and Winston, 1960)

Scully, Roger, *Elections in Wales* (Cardiff: University of Wales Press, 2017)

Seyd, Patrick and Whiteley, Paul, *Labour's Grass Roots* (Oxford: Clarendon Press, 1992)

Sides, John, 'Democrats are gay, Republicans are rich: Our stereotypes of political parties are amazingly wrong' [https://www.washingtonpost.com/news/monkey-cage/wp/2016/05/23/democrats-are-gay-republicans-are-rich-our-stereotypes-of-political-parties-are-amazingly-wrong/] (23 May 2016)

Sides, John and Vavreck, Lynn, *The Gamble* (Princeton, NJ: Princeton University Press, 2014)

Singh, Matt, 'Is there a shy Tory factor in 2015?' [http://www.ncpolitics.uk/2015/05/shy-tory-factor-2015.html/] (6 May 2015)

— —, 'Where the polls went wrong' [http://www.ncpolitics.uk/2015/11/where-the-polls-went-wrong.html] (18 November 2015)

Slovic, Paul, 'Perceived Risk, Trust and Democracy', in Cvetovich, George and Löftstedt, Ragnar E. (eds), *Social Trust and the Management of Risk* (Oxford and New York: Earthscan, 1999), pp. 42–52

Sobolewska, Maria, 'Party Strategies, Political Opportunity Structure and the Descriptive Representation of Ethnic Minorities in Britain', *West European Politics* (2013), vol. 36, no. 3, pp. 615–33

Soroka, Stuart N., *Negativity in Democratic Politics* (Cambridge: Cambridge University Press, 2014)

Southwell, Patricia, 'Political Alienation: Behavioural Implications of Efficacy and Trust in the 2008 US Presidential Election', *Review of European Studies* (2012), vol. 4, no. 2, pp. 71–7

Stimson, James A., *Public Opinion in America: Moods, Cycles, and Swings* (Boulder, CO: Westview Press, 1991)

Sturgis, Patrick, Baker, Nick, Callegaro, Mario, Fisher, Stephen, Green, Jane, Jennings, Will, Kuha, Jouni, Lauderdale, Ben and Smith, Patten, *Report of the Inquiry into the 2015 British General Election Opinion Polls* (London: Market Research Society and British Polling Council, 2016)

Sturgis, Patrick, Brunton-Smith, Ian, Read, Sanna and Allum, Nick, 'Does Ethnic Diversity Erode Trust? Putnam's "Hunkering Down" Thesis Reconsidered', *British Journal of Political Science* (2011), vol. 41, no. 1, pp. 57–82

Takeda, Hiroko, 'Gender-Related Social Policy' in Gaunder, Alisa (ed), *The Routledge Handbook of Japanese Politics* (London and New York: Routledge, 2011), pp. 212–23

Theocharis, Yannis, 'Cuts, Tweets, Solidarity and Mobilisation: How the Internet Shaped the Student Occupations', *Parliamentary Affairs* (2012), vol. 65, no. 1, pp. 162–94

Tilley, James, 'We Don't Do God? Religion and Party Choice in Britain', *British Journal of Political Science* (2015), vol. 45, no. 4, pp. 907–27

Vigen, Tyler, *Spurious Correlations* (New York and Boston: Hachette Books, 2015)

Wald, Kenneth, *Crosses on the Ballot* (Princeton, NJ: Princeton University Press, 1983)

Wall, Matthew, Sudulich, Maria Laura and Cunningham, Kevin, 'What Are the Odds? Using Constituency-level Betting Markets to Forecast Seat Shares in the 2010 UK General Elections', *Journal of Elections, Public Opinion and Parties* (2012), vol. 22, no. 1, pp. 3–26

Wallas, Graham, *Human Nature in Politics* (New Brunswick, NJ: Transaction Books, [1908] 1981)

Whiteley, Paul, 'Is the Party Over? The Decline of Party Activism and Membership across the Democratic World', *Party Politics* (2011), vol. 17, no. 1, pp. 21–44

Whiteley, Paul, Clarke, Harold D., Sanders, David and Stewart, Marianne C.,

Affluence, Austerity and Electoral Change in Britain (Oxford: Oxford University Press, 2013)

Wlezien, Christopher, 'The Public as Thermostat: Dynamics of Preferences for Spending', *American Journal of Political Science* (1995), vol. 39, no. 4, pp. 981–1000

Wlezien, Christopher and Erikson, Robert S., 'The Timeline of Presidential Election Campaigns', *Journal of Politics* (2002), vol. 64, no. 4, pp. 969–93

Wlezien, Christopher, Jennings, Will, Fisher, Stephen, Ford, Robert and Pickup, Mark, 'Polls and the Vote in Britain', *Political Studies* (2013), vol. 61, s. 1, pp. 66–91

Zarycki, Tomasz, 'History and Regional Development: A Controversy over the "Right" Interpretation of the Role of History in the Development of the Polish Regions', *Geoforum* (2007), vol. 38, no. 3, pp. 485–93

Index

France 67, 160, 161, 162, 204, 247–51
fraud 54
Front National (FN) 247–8, 249–50

gambling 77–81
gender 121–32, 261–4
general elections xii–xv, 19–22, 122,
    205; *see also* 2015 election
geography 10–11, 85–6, 233–6
Germany 228, 229–30, 257–9, 264
Global Corruption Barometer (GCB)
    163
Goldsmith, Zac 179
grassroots networks 199, 200
Green Party 34, 86, 112, 173
Greenpeace 209
Guardian (newspaper) 9, 92, 93

Hague, William 103
happiness 283–6
Hayden Phillips Review 164, 165
health 97; *see also* National Health
    Service (NHS)
Howard, Michael 103
hypocrisy 160, 162

identity politics 239
immigration 34, 39, 98–100, 102–3,
    113
    and distrust 105–9, 145
    and the EU 269–72

and representation 135–8
and USA 237–9, 240
income tax 154
India 67, 127
internet 71–5
intolerance 91–4
Iraq war 143
Ireland 28, 241–4
issues 97–100, 101–4
Italy 74

Japan 261–4
Johnson, Boris 179

Khan, Sadiq 179
Kinnock, Neil 193

Labour Party xiv, 3–4, 111, 114
    and class 117–19
    and economics 22
    and ethnic minorities 37, 40, 228
    and immigration 107
    and issue ownership 97, 100, 103
    and leadership xv, 204, 275–8
    and membership 199, 200, 201
    and religion 26, 28, 29
    and safe seats 85, 86
    and target groups 10, 11–12
    and Wales 193
    see also New Labour
Lammert, Norbert 258

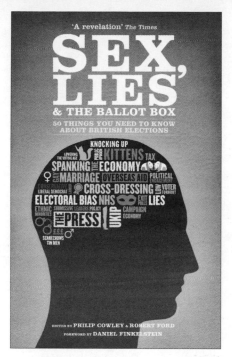